I0441921

ELBERT COUNTY, GEORGIA INFERIOR COURT MINUTES

February 4, 1791 - July 14, 1801

By
Michael A. Ports

CLEARFIELD

Copyright © 2015
Michael A. Ports
All Rights Reserved

Reprinted for Clearfield Company by
Genealogical Publishing Company
Baltimore, Maryland
2015

ISBN 978-0-8063-5783-6

Introduction

On December 10, 1790, the Georgia General Assembly created Elbert County, from a portion of Wilkes County, making Elberton the seat of its new government. The Inferior Court, made up of five justices of the peace for the county, tried any civil case except those involving title to land. The Inferior Court had jurisdiction over county business matters, such as care for the poor, building and maintaining the courthouse and jail, building and maintaining roads and bridges, establishing ferries, issuing licenses to sell liquor, appointing guardians, nominating justices of the peace and constables, authorizing indentures, and maintaining a register of wills. The Clerk of the Inferior Court kept minutes of its various proceedings.

The first volume of Inferior Court Minutes begins February 4, 1791 and continues through July 14, 1801. The following transcription comes from the microfilm of the original record book made in 1960 for the Genealogical Society of Salt Lake City, Utah and the Georgia Department of Archives and History. The original volume includes a partial index of plaintiffs, guardians, and selected appointments, that is not transcribed here. Instead, a full name index follows the transcription. The clerk entered consecutive numbers in the upper right hand corner of only the right hand pages, thus making the page numbers indicate two pages, the right hand page with the number and the adjacent left hand page. The numbers between brackets [ ] are the original page numbers. The transcription places three underscores ___ in the upper left hand corner of each left hand page, allowing the reader to determine which original page number should be associated with any particular minute book entry. The clerk entered page number 16 on two consecutive right hand pages and skipped the number 20 when entering the page numbers. The clerk neglected to number the right hand page between pages 46 and 47.

Middleton Woods apparently served as the Inferior Court Clerk during the entire period covered by the first volume of minutes, but neglected to sign all of the proceedings at the end of each day. An analysis of the handwriting indicates that the minutes are in the handwriting of at least four different men; yet, seven men, Samuel Blackburn, P. Early, John Griffin, J. Huntington, John Mathews, John C. Watson, and M. Williamson, signed the minute book attesting to the accuracy of at least one entry. The seven men may have been deputy clerks or possibly attorneys. For the most part, the handwriting is legible, making the transcription straightforward and not too difficult. The occasional ink smear or other imperfection is noted in brackets, for example [smear] or [illegible].

Sometimes the line crossing the letter "t" is faint or missing entirely, making it appear to be the letter "l." Sometimes the line crossing the letter "t" extends across the entire word, making any letters "l" in the word appear to be the letter "t." In a similar fashion, sometimes the dot over the letter "i" is too faint or missing, making it appear to be the letter "e." At least one clerk makes the letters "a" and "o" in a similar manner, while another forms the letters "a" and "u" similarly. The flourish at the end of some words can look like the letter "s." The capital letters "L" and "S" sometimes can be difficult to distinguish. Also, the clerks formed the capital letters "I" and "J" identically. Determining which letter usually is straightforward when the first letter of a name, but entirely a guess when a middle initial. The various clerks almost never used an apostrophe to indicate a possessive. The transcription follows Sperry's recommended guidelines for reading early script.[1] Readers are encouraged to consult the original court minutes or the microfilm copy either to confirm the transcription or formulate alternative interpretations of the clerks' handwriting. Occasionally, the clerk crossed out a word, phrase, or even an entire entry, those deleted entries included herein.

The transcription does not correct any spelling or grammar, no matter how obvious the errors, but does add a few commas and periods for clarity. For the most part, the transcription maintains the general format of the minutes, but presents lists of jurors in a standard numbered format. The clerks entered a squiggly vertical line to delineate lawsuit citations and other headings, duplicated by the symbol } in the transcription. In all but two instances, the clerk entered the capital letter X to indicate the mark of a person unable to write, Thomas Barren using the capital letter "B" and Sylvanus Stokes using the capital letter "C."

The book is dedicated to the memory of William Blake, John and Martha (Moon) Blake, Jacob and Caty Eberhart, David and Susannah (Griffith) Eberhart, James and Isabella (Rhea) McCleskey, William and Sarah Moon, William and Margaret (Harbin) Suttle, Isaac and Sarah Suttle, and Samuel and Elizabeth (Patton) Woods, all early residents of Elbert County and just a few of the author's numerous Georgia ancestors. Many thanks are offered to Joe Garonzik, of the Genealogical Publishing Company, for his sound advice and counsel. Very special thanks are offered Marcia Tremonti for her continued patience and encouragement during this challenging endeavor.

---

[1] Sperry, Kip, *Reading Early American Handwriting.* Genealogical Publishing Company, Inc., Baltimore, Maryland, Sixth Printing, 2008.

Inferior Court Minutes 1791-1801

Inferior County Court began and held In and for the County of Elbert, Thursday, the [1]
twenty fourth day February, in the year one Thousand Seven hundred and ninety one, at the house of Mr Thomas Carter.

Present, the honorable William Barnett, Evan Ragland, James Tait, Richardson Hunt, esquires

Audley Maxwell }
vs } Case
The Administrators of }
John Bowen, dec^{d} }

The defendants came into court and confessed Judgment for the sum of One hundred and twenty pounds, to be discharged upon the delivery of two likely negroes, not to be under the age of fifteen years, nor over twenty five, with stay of execution untill the first day of December next.

John Mathews, P. D.

The following persons were drawn to serve as petit Jurors for May Term 1791.

No
1. Absolam Kilgore
2. Joseph Moulder
3. Joseph Underwood
4. James Butler
5. Benj^{a} Fleming
6. Thomas Heard
7. Abraham Myers
8. James McLire
9. Lewis Lugget
10. William Howington
11. James Hammock
12. William Jennings
13. Solomon Patton
14. Martain

——

16. Lewis Moseley
17. William Taylor
18. Ezekiel Cloud
19. Dudley Cook
20. Abraham Colson
21. John Royal
22. Absolam Davis
23. William Brown
24. George Aberhard
25. Robert Thompson
27. William Clark
28. William Adkins
29. Oliver Rock
30. Stephen Gardner
31. John Tweedle
32. Isaac Morris
33. Boling Clark
34. Nathl Beddingfild
35. James McDonald
36. James Crow

William Huntsman }
vs } covenant
Isham Thompson }

The Plaintiff appearing and acknowledged that the Debt was discharged. Ordered, that The Suit be dismissed.

Ordered, that John Davis, Edward Clark, Robert Taylor, and William Hansford be appointed Constables, upon their being qualified.

John Moore }
vs } Case
Charles Kenedy }

Issue Joined and Continued.

William Sutton }
vs } Debt
Andrew Johnston }

Issue Joined & Continued.

Claybourn Sandwich } [2]
Assee Robert Pullum }
vs } Debt
Evan Ragland & }
George Turman, Exe[rs] }
Jacob Colson }

Issue Joined & Continued.

John Simpson }
vs } Case
David McCleskey }

issue Joined & continued.

James Coleman }
vs } Case
James Curin }

issue Joined & continued.

William Martin }
vs } Case
Hugh McDonald }

issue Joined & continued.

Dionysius Oliver }
vs } debt
Isham Thompson }

issue Joined & Continued.

Thomas Carter, appl }
vs }
Isham Thompson, Resp[s] }

Continued.

William Moss, appl[t] }
vs }
John Barnett, Resp[s] }

Continued.

Thomas Carter, appl }
vs }
Isham Thompson, Res[p] }

On motion of M[r] Blackburn, Ordered, that A dedimus potistatum

---

do issue, to South Carolina, to take the deposition of George Claudus, before Patrick Calhound and Adam C. Jones, esquires, in the County of Abeville, in said State, in behalf of the aapplicant, which deposition shall be taken in evidence in this Court of Returned duly sealed up and delivered to the Clerk of said Court, on or before the third Thursday in May next, the opposit party having ten days previous notice, said deposition to be taken the Second Monday in April next, at the house of Patrick Calhound, esq[r].

Red & Recv[d] W[m] Barnett

May 19th 1791

The Court Met agreeable to adjournment.

Wm Barnett, James Tate, Evin Ragland, Richardson Hunt

On Motion of Mr Thomas Carter, Ordered, that he be admitted to Retail Spirituous liquors and keep a Tavern, during the time the Superior & Inferior Courts shall be held at his house, he paying for such licence in proportion to the time he keeps such Tavern.

On Motion of Walker Richardson, Ordered, that the said Richardson be allowed a lycence to keep Tavern at the House where he now

lives, he giving bond and security, as the Law directs. [3]

John Barnett, Res^t }
vs } appeal
William Moss, appl }

No 2 Jury Sworn. (to wit)

1. Absolam Kilgore
2. Joseph Moulder
3. Joseph Underwood
4. James Butler
5. Lewis Gegget
6. William Howington
7. Lewis Moseley
8. Dudley Cook
9. Richard Nubanks
10. George Aberhart
11. Abraham Cohon
12. John Royal

Respondents Evidence, John Rogers, Thos B. Scott

app^l Evidence, John Gorham

We the Jury find for the applicant.

Joseph Moulder, F. M.

Clayborn Sandwich }
Assee Robert Pullum }
vs } Debt
Evan Ragland & }
George Turner, Exe^rs }
of Jacob Cohon }

The Jury Sworn, to wit.

1. Oliver Rock
2. John Twedle
3. John Patterson
7. Isaac Morris
8. William Watkins
9. John Tureman

4. John Coleman
5. James Crow
6. Thomas Colbert
10 Thomas Cook
11. Joel Butler
12. Boling Clark

Plaintiffs evidence, John Coleman & Wm Hatcher.

We the Jury find for the Plaintiff the sum of the note & lawful interest, amounting to ten pounds, Sixteen Shillings.

Wm Watkins, M. F.

John Simpson }
vs } Case
David McCleskey }

The same Jury as in the Case Barnett vs Moss.

We the Jury agree that David McCleskey do pay the principal, with lawful interest & Costs.

Joseph Moler, F. M.

The Court adjourned till ten o'Clock tomorrow.

Friday Morning

The Court met agreeable to adjournment.

Present, the honorable William Barnett, Evin Ragland, Richardson Hunt, esquires.

Isham Thompson, Res^{pt} }
vs } No 1 appeal
Thomas Carter, App^{l} }

Jury Sworn, to wit.

1. Oliver Rock
2. James Butler
3. Lewis Liggit
4. Lewis Moseley
5. Dudley Cook
6. John Tweedle
7. James Crow
8. Absolom Davis
9. Joseph Molder
10. George Averhart
11. Thomas Colbert
12. Isaac Moriss

Respondants Evidence }
Julias Howard }
James Carter }

Appl Evidence
George Claudus

We the Jury do agree & find for the Plaintiff five pouns & Costs, with stay of execution.

Robert Pulliam, Secty. Joseph Molin, F. M.

John Lindsey } [4]
vs } Case
William Cartin }

Issue Joined & Continued.

N° 1.

William Muncrief }
vs } Covenant
John Turman }

issue Joined & Continued.

N° 2.

Israel Pickins }
vs } Debt
William Eliott & }
John McCurdy }

Issue Joined & Continued.

N° 4.

William McKindley }
vs } Case
William Daniel }

issue Joined & Continued.

N° 5.

James Jett }
vs } debt
John Rogers }

Dismised at the Defendants Costs.

N° 6.

John Patterson }
vs } Case
William Daniel }

Issue Joined & Continued.

N° 8.

S. C. Linuor & Wm Hutson }
vs } Case
Walker Richardson }

Settled.

N° 9.

Micajah McGehee }
vs } Debt
Andrew Jonston }

Issue Joined & Cont^d.

N° 10.

Abreham Livingston }
vs } Debt
Andrew Jonston }

Issue Joined & Continued.

N° 11.

William Bredd }
vs } Debt
William Elliott }

issue Joined & Continued.

N° 12.

Peter Carnes & }
Thos P. Carnes }
vs } Case
William Daniel }

issue Joind & Continued.

N° 13.

William Gardner }
vs } Debt
David McCleskey }

issue Joind & Continued.

N° 14.

Thos P. Carnes }
vs } Case
John Depriest & }
John Cosby }

issue Joined & Continued.

N° 15.

William Head }
vs } Case
Isham Thompson }

issue Joind & Continued.

N° 16 [5]

John Hightower }
vs } case
Anthony Haney }

issue Joind & Continued.

N° 17.

Gideon Booker }
vs } trespass on the Case
Thomas Carter }

issue Joind & Continued.

N° 18.

John Dunn }
vs } debt
William Daniel }

issue Joind & Continued.

N° 19.

William Watkins }
vs } Covenant
Isham Thompson & }
John Thompson }

N° 20.

Thomas C. Russell }
vs } Case
William Stokes }

issue Joined & Continued.

N° 22.

William Moss }
vs } Case
William Daniel }

issue Joind & Continued.

N° 24.
the Commissioners of }
the town of Washington }
vs } Debt
John Gorham & }
John Jonston }

—

Issue Joind & Continued.

N° 25.

Charles Cosby }
vs } Debt
William Moss }

issue Joind & Continued.

N° 26.

M. Maher & C° }
vs } Case
Charles Kennedy }

dismissed at the plaintiffs Cost.

N° 27.

William Shorter }
vs } Assault & Battery
David McCleskey et al }

issue Joind & Contn[d].

N° 29.

Isham Thompson }
vs } Covenant
William Moss }

issue Joind & Continued.

N° 30.

John R. Ragland }
vs } Assun[t]
William Moss, esq[r] }

N° 31.

William Allen }
vs } Debt
Joseph M. Russell }

Dismissed at the Plaintiffs Cost.

James Jett }
vs } Debt
John Rogers }

N° 5. Judgment Confessed.

John Dunn } [6]
vs } debt
William Daniel }

upon the motion of Mr Mathews, attorney for the Plaintiff, Ordered, that a didimus potistatum do issue to the County of Roan, in North Carolina, to take the examination of Michael Brown & Harry Arinhard, Witnesses for the Plaintiff, in the above Suit, which examination is to be taken at the house of the aforesaid Michael Brown, on the tenth day of July next, before any two of three three nearest Residing Magistrates to the house of the above mentioned Michael Brown, and that the said examination, when so taken, be transmited to this Court, on the Third Thursday in August next, where the Court of Elbert shall then be held, the same to be certified, under the hand and seales of the said Magistrates, and transmited to us sealed up, the said Plaintiff giving to the opposit party or his council fifteen days previous Notice of the time & place of taking such examination.

Mathews, Plff Atty

Mathias Mahar }
vs } No 26 Case
Charles Kennedy }

Dismissed at the defendants cost.

Thomas Carter }
vs } Covenant
Garrard Walthall }

The defendant, Jerred Walthall, came into court & confessed for five pounds eleven shillings & nine pence half penny specia, with costs of suit, & interest till paid, with six months stay of execution.

May 29th 1791

Garrad Walthall
Blackburn, Plff Atty

James Coleman }
vs } Special action on the case.
James Currin }

Continued to the next Court at the defendants Cost.

William Martain }
vs }
Hugh McDonald }

Jury Sworn, to wit.

1. John Hubberd
2. A. Colison
3. Thomas Cook
4. Wamack Blankinship
5. Thomas Colbert
6. Absolam Kilgore
7. John Oliver
8. Martin Ferrell
9. Garrad Walthall
10. John Royall
11. William Howington
12. Richd Newbank

We the Jury, say that the Plaintiff Receive Woods note & pay Costs of Suit.

John Oliver, F. M.

Micajah McGehee } [7]
vs }
Andrew Johnston }

William Johnston, being Bail for the defendant, rendered him up to the Court & was Released from his bail bond & Remains in Custody of the Sheriff, untill Special Bail be given.

Claybourn Sandwich }
Assee of Robert Pulliam }
vs } Debt
Evan Ragland & }
George Turman, exetrs }
of Jacob Cohon }

Isham Thompson comes into Court & enters himself security for the stay of execution agreeable to Law.

Thomas C. Russell }
vs } Attachment
John Cunningham } Inquiry

Jury Sworn, to wit. The same as in the Case Thompson vs Carter.

We the Jury find for Tho[s] C. Russell £7,9,5, with costs of suit.

Joseph Moulder, F. M.

The Excts of R. Aycock }
in behalf of the estate }
of D. Hinton }
vs } Attachment
John Cunningham } Inquiry

the same Jury as in the above Russell vs Cunningham.

We the Jury find for the Plaintiff £31 & Cost of suit.

Joseph Moulder, F. M.

Julias Howard }
vs } Attachment
John Cunningham } Writ Inquiry

The same Jury as in the two before.

We the Jury find for the Plaintiff Twelve pounds, two shillings, & Cost of Suit, with lawful interest.

Joseph Moulder, F. M.

The following persons were drawn for Jurors for August term.

1. Archelus Walker
2. Benj[n] Tolman
3. John Baker
4. John Shackelford
5. James Lawry
6. W[m] Brawner
7. W[m] Speares
8. John Brazell
18. Jesse Goss
19. Reuben White
20. Thomas Burton, J[r]
21. Nathan Jones
22. Absolom Hooper
23. Smith Cook
24. Thomas Burk
25. Hillery Hendrick

9. James Oliver	26. John McCiavin
10. Andrew Hemphill	27. Richard Coulter, Jr
11. Thomas Burk	28. Thomas Webb
12. Jesse Baker	29. Francis Guttery
13. John Davis	30. William Brown
14. Benj[a] Brown	31. William McConnell
15. Robert Cowdon	32. Joseph Henderson
16. Miredy Brown	33. Zach Butler
17. Elijah Mullins	34. Daniel Reaves
35. Bridger Haney	36. Henry Rose

[8]

Thomas Owins }
vs }
Daniel Stalker }
& Evan Ragland }

Nonsuit for want of & illegality of the writ.

Ordered, that the Clerk issue citations for each defaulting Juror to shew cause at the next Court why they should not be fined, as the law directs.

On Motion of M[r] Benjamin Ragland, it is ordered that lycence be granted to said Ragland to keep a Tavern, his giving bond agreeable to Law and paying the fees.

Micajah McGehee }
vs }
Andrew Johnston }

Elijah Miller comes into Court & acknowledges himself bound in the Sum of thirty pounds, as Special Bail for the defendant, Rec[d] by Blackburn, the plaintiffs Atty.

W[m] Barnett, R. Hunt, Evan Ragland

The Court then adjourned till Court in course.

Attest. Middleton Woods, Clk E. C.

At an Inferior Court, begun, held & continued at the dweling house of M[r] Thomas Carter.

18th day of August 1791

Present, the honorable William Barnett, Evin Ragland, Richardson Hunt, James Tait, Esqr[s]

The Court proceeded to the choice of three Inspectors for Olivers Ware House in said County, When the following persons were unanimously appointed, to wit. Thomas Burton, Senr, John Oliver & Dionysius Oliver, Senr, and they came into Court and entered into bond, according to Law.

Lucy Abbet came into court and made choice of Walker Richardson as her Guardian.

Sarrah Smith came into court and made choice of James McCleskey as her Guardian.

William Sutton }
vs } debt
Andrew Johnson }

Judgment Confessed for nine pounds, thirteen shillings, with five months stay of execution, on Security given.

Blackburn, def. Atty

James Coleman }
vs } Case
James Currin }

Jury Sworn, to wit.

1. Archabald Walker
2. William Brown
3. James Oliver
4. Andrew Hemphill
5. Thomas Burk
6. John Davis
7. Benjn Brown
8. Miredy Brown
9. Jesse Goss
10. Reuben White
11. Smith Cook
12. Thomas Burk

[9]

We the Jury find for the Plaintiff £28,9,0¼, with the Cost of suit.

Arch^d Walker, M. F.

John Oliver entered himself Security.

John Lindsey }
vs } Case
William Carter }

Jury Sworn, to wit.

1. Hillery Hendrick	7. Robert Cosby
2. Richard Coulter	8. Jesse Thompson
3. Thomas Webb	9. John Terrell
4. Joseph Henderson	10. William Head
5. Zachariah Butler	11. John Shackelford
6. Henry Rose	12. Thomas Burton

We the Jury find for the defendant.

W[m] Head, F. M.

William Muncrief }
vs } Cov[t]
John Tureman }

Jury Sworn, to wit.

1. Archabald	7. Mirody Brown
2. William Brawner	8. Jesse Goss
3. James Oliver	9. Reuben White
4. Andrew Hemphill	10. Smith Cook
5. Thomas Burke	11. Thomas Cook
6. John Davis	12. John Hubbard

We the Jury find for the Plaintiff £13,4,6, with lawful interest & cost.

Arch[d] Walker, F. M.

William Haley entered himself security.

William B[illegible] }
vs } Debt
William Elliott }

The defendant came into court & confessed Judgment for the sum of Eight Pounds, with interest agreeable to note, with five moths stay of execution, untill paid. Robert Corethers, Secuirty.

Walker, def[t] Atty

Micajah McGehee }
vs } debt
Andrew Johnson }

Judgment confessed for fifteen pounds, with Interest untill paid, with stay of Levy five months & Cost of suit.

Churchill, atty for def[t]

Peter Carnes & }
Tho[s] P. Carnes }
vs } Case
William Daniel }

The same Jury as in the last Suit.

We the Jury find for the Plaintiff £6,,18, with lawful interest & Cost.

Archibald Walker, F. M.

William McKindley }
vs } Case
William Daniel }

The defendant came into court & confessed judgment for thirteen pounds, fourteen shillings, with stay of execution five months, on security being given, which may be discharged upon the payment of six & twenty hundred pounds of Tobacco of the Petersburg inspector, on or before the 25th of November

next, the said Daniels paying all legal costs. [10]

August 18th 1791

Samuel Blackburn, def[t] Atty

The Court then adjourned untill ten o'Clock to Morrow.

W[m] Barnett, Evan Ragland, James Tait

Attest. M. Woods, Clk

Friday, 19th of August 1791

The Court Met agreeable to adjournment.

Present, the honorable William Barnett, James Tait, Evin Ragland, Richardson Hunt, Esquires

Ordered, that the following Jurors be fined an half dollar each, to wit.

John Shackelford, William Brawner, James Oliver, Andrew Hemphill, John Davis, Absolom Hooper, Thomas Burke, Richard Coulter, Francis Guttery, William Brown, the above Jury attended and was excused, Absolom Hooper excepted.

John Dunn }
vs } Debt
William Daniel }

David McCleskey came into court & entered himself Security.

—

[illegible] that William Daniel Confess Judgment for the sum of sixty pounds, with costs of suit and stay of execution for five months, upon giving security, which sum of sixty pounds may be discharged by said Daniel making titles to as much of the following tract of Land, as shall by disinterested men be adjudged to be worth the said sum in ready money cash, the Land lying on Cedar Creek, a branch of Oconey, Containing one thousand acres, granted to Nimrod Long & should the persons chosen not agree upon the price of said, an apprise to be chosen by them.

Blackburn, def^t atty

Mathews, Plff Atty

The Commissioners of }
the Town of Washington }
vs } Debt
John Gorham & }
John Johnson }

The defendant came into court & confessed Judgment for the ~~sum~~ Specialty, with Interest till paid, with Six months Stay of execution, on security being given.

Huntington for Walker atty def.

Wm Stokes entered himself security for stay of execution.

Charles Cosby }
vs } Debt
William Moss, esqr. }

I appear for the defendant, William Moss, and confess Judgment for five pounds, with interest for four years, with stay of levy five months,

Security being given, and costs of suit. [11]

Blackburn, def[t] atty

Anthony Haney came into court and entered himself Security of the process.

Samuel Nelson }
vs } Attachment
John Watson }

Jury sworn, to wit.

1. Archabald Walker	7. Jesse Goss
2. William Brawner	8. Reuben White
3. Thomas Burke	9. Smith Cook
4. John Davis	10. H. Hendricks
5. Benj[n] Brown	11. Rich[d] Coulter
6. Merody Brown	12. Thomas Webb

We the Jury find for the Plaintiff the sum of twenty five pounds, with Costs.

Arch[d] Walker, F. M.

Israel Pickens }
vs } Debt
William Elliott & }
John McCurdy }

The defendant came into court and confessed Judgment for thirty two pounds, fourteen shillings & ten pence, with Cost & five months stay of execution.

Robert Coruthers came into Court and acknowledged himself Security.

John Hightower }
vs } Case
Anthony Haney }

William Moss acknowledged himself Security.

---

the same Jury as in the Case Sam[l] Nelson vs John Watson.

We the Jury find for the Plaintiff Six pounds & Cost.

Arch[d] Walker, F. M.

Thomas C. Russell }
vs } Case
William Stokes }

Saml Nelson entered himself Security.

The defendant, by Saml Blackburn, his attorney, confesses Judgment for the sum of seven pounds, eighteen shillings, & six pence, with costs & Interest untill paid, and stay of levy for five Months.

S. Blackburn, def^{t} Atty

Abraham Livingston }
vs } Debt
Andrew Johnson }

The defendant came into court & confessed Judgment for twenty five pounds, Seven shillings, with cost of suit, & stay of execution five months, on security being given.

Churchill, Atty for def^{t}

Collin Reed }
vs } Attachment
John Cuningham }

The same jury as in the last jury cause.

We the Jury find for the Plaintiff five pounds, four shillings, & ten pence, with Cost.

A. Walker, F. M.

William Shorter } [12]
vs } Assumsit
David McCleskey }

The Jury Sworn (to wit)

1. Archabald Walker
2. Wm Brawner
3. James Oliver
4. Thomas Burke
5. Reuben White
6. Jesse Goss
7. Benjn Brown
8. Merody Brown
9. Smith Cook
10. Hillery Hendricks
11. Richard Coulter
12. Thomas Webb

We the Jury find for the Plaintiff Eighteen pounds & Eight pence & Cost.

Tho. Cook entered himself security.

Arch[d] Walker, F. M.

Sam[l] Gardner }
vs } debt
David McCleskey }

The defendant came into court and confessed Judgment for the sum of ten pounds, sixteen shillings, with Costs, and stay of execution five months.

Mathews, Pltff Atty

Robert Wasden }
vs } assault & Battery
David McCleskey }

the Jury, as in the last cause.

We the Jury find for the plaintiff nine pence.

A. Walker, F. M.

Court adjourned till 9 o'clock tomorrow.

Attest. M. Wood, Clk W[m] Barnett, Evan Ragland, Ja[s] Tait

Saturday, 20th of August 1791

Court Met agreeable to adjournment.

Present, the honorable William Barnett, James Tait, Even Ragland, Richardson Hunt, esquires

Charles Cosby }
vs }
Jesse Thompson }

Settled.

W[m] Hayes }
vs }
Hugh McDonald }

Issue Joind.

Leonard Marbury }
vs }
Job Hammond Wilcox }

Settled.

David Adams }
vs } Case
John Parton, et al }

Issue Joind.

Order for dedimus to issue to Burke County, North Carolina to take the deposition of Susanna Martain, a witness for the defendants, to be taken at the court house of said County, on the third monday in October next, before three of the nearest magistrates to said court house.

Blackburn, Deft Atty

Sampson Dickinson } [13]
vs }
Tho[s] C. Russell }

Settled.

Stewart Hays & Co. }
vs }
Thomas C. Russell }

Issue Joind.

Sam[l] Willison }
vs }
Benj[a] Cook }

Issue Joind.

William Elliott }
vs }
Hugh McDonald }
& John King }

Issue Joind.

Thomas Walton }
vs }
Benjamin Ragland }

issue Joind.

E. Wambersie }
vs }
Hugh McDonald }

The Plaintiff being called and not appearing, was nonsuited.

Elizabeth Rutherford }
by Banj[a] Rutherford }
her next friend }
vs }
Edward McGarrey }

Issue Joind.

William Elliott }
vs } Covenant
Bradock M. Don & }
William Flanekin }

Judgment by default.

Thomas Walton }
vs }
James Curren }

Issue Joind.

Joseph Nail }
vs } Case
Jesse Casey, et al }

Judgment by default.

Larkin Gatewood }
vs } Trespass vi at armas
James Carter }

Issue Joind.

Dionysius Oliver }
vs } Case
John F. Thompson}

Settled.

The following persons were drawn as Jurors for November Term, to wit.

1. Nathan Bonds
2. Clem Wilkins
3. William Head
4. John Buckhanon
5. William Guttery
6. David Nelloms
7. Bossen Brown
8. Abel House
9. Robert Kenneday
10. John Ress
11. Joseph Williams
12. Sam[l] Moss
13. Richard Coulter
14. John Turell
15. Edward Clarke
16. W[m] Edward
17. Josiah Cook
18. John Coleman
19. John Giles
20. Thomas Pum
21. Arch[d] Smith
22. Sam[l] Tyner
23. Joseph Deadwider
24. John Blake
25. James Pattern
26. Thomas Hodges
27. Rich[d] Dodd

28. John Wilkins [14]
29. Gilbert Borden
30. Jessee Dodd
31. John Buckhanon
32. Jacob Durham
33. George Russell
34. Joseph Martin
35. Stephen Westbrook

Robert Chambers }
vs } Case
Archer Smith }

issue Joind.

Barkley Martin }
vs } Case
William Carter }

Issue Joind.

Henry Carlton }
vs } Cov[t]
Hugh Flanekin }
& Hugh Saxton }

Issue Joind.

Thomas Owen }
vs } Covenant
Daniel Stalker }
& Evan Ragland }

Issue Joind.

Elijah Owen }
vs } Debt
William Elliott }

Case to plead next Court. Continued without plea untill next Term.

Mary Kerr }
vs } Debt
John & W[m] Turke }

Issue Joind.

Joseph Dobbs }
vs } Case
Charles Hutchings }

issue Joind.

Elijah Owen }
vs }
Joseph M. Russell }

Issue Joind. Judgment by default.

James Huling }
vs } Debt
William Carter }

issue.

William Smith }
vs } Case
Jacob Whitworth }

leave to plead & try Next Term.

Thomas C. Russell }
vs } debt
Hugh McDonald & }
John Cunningham }

Issue Joined.

Moses Trimble }
vs } Case
John Luckie }

Judgment by default.

Thomas C. Russell }
vs } Case
Christopher Harris & }
Jesse Newby }

Issue Joined.

Peter Carnes }
vs } Case
William Moss, esq[r] }

William Grimes } [15]
vs } debt
Hugh McDonald }

Issue Joind.

Joseph Hawthan }
vs } Assault & Battery
Thomas Lovelady }
et al }

left to refrence.

Sam[l] Hunter }
vs }
William Elliott }

Settled.

William Elliott }
vs }
Sam[l] Hunter }

Settled.

John Depriest }
vs } debt
William Carter }

Issue Joind.

Josias Jones }
vs } Trover
Sam[l] Blackburn }

On Motion of M[r] Mathews, Attorney for Plaintiff, Ordered that dedimus do issue to the County of Buckingham, In Virginia, to take the examination of Col[o] Joseph Cable, Thomas Sanders, & William Perkins, Jun[r], Witnesses for the Plaintiff, and that a Commission to Joseph Cable, Jur., Common Glover, & Charles Moseley, or any two of them, and if they cannot

---

be found, to any two Magistrates within the said County of Buckingham, to take the examination of said Witnesses, at the house of Josias Jones, the Plaintiff, or at any other convenient place in the County, and that the same be returned sealed up to this Court, on the fourth Thursday in November next.

Mathews, Ptff Atty

Thomas C. Russell }
vs } Case
Jarrad Walthall }

Issue Joind.

Micajah Clark }
vs } Case
William Carter & }
Tho[s] B. Scott }

Issue Joind.

Abolom Jackson }
vs } Case
William Carter }

Issue Joind.

Josias Jones }
vs } Trover & Conversion
Isaac Suttles }
Wife & }
W[m] Moore }

Issue Joind. Ordered that a Dedimus issue.

Upon motion of M[r] Mathews, attorney for the Plff, Ordered that a dedimus do issue to the County of Buckingham, in Virginia, to take the examination of Col[o] Joseph Cable, Thomas Saunders, & William Perkins, Jun.,

Witnesses for the Plaintiff, and that a Commission do issue to Joseph Cable, Ju[n], Edmon [16] Glover, & Charles Moseley, or any two of them (and if they cannot be found) to any magistrates within the County of Buckingham, to take the examination of said Witnesses, at the house of Josias Jones, the Plaintiff, or at any other Convenient place within the County, and that the same be returned sealed up to this Court, on the fourth Thursday of November next.

Mathews, Ptff Atty

Richard Smith }
& Thomas Napier }
vs } Ejectment
William Stiles & }
Thomas Cook }

Nonsuit. M. Chiselom enter himself Security.

William Payton }
vs } Attachment
George Johnson }

Judgment by default.

John Oliver }
vs } Debt
Henry Rose }

Issue Joind.

On Motion of Mr Huntington, Attorney for the defendant, it Ordered that a dedimus potistatum do issue to Justices of the peace for the County of Granville, to take the examination of Wm Suart, of the State of North Carolina, according to the interogations here in Court filed, & hereunto annexed.

Ordered, that the following Rules be observed by persons who have or may obtain Licence to Keep a Tavern in said County of Elbert, to Wit.

For a dinner	£0,7,6
Do Breakfast	1,2
Do Supper	1,2
Do Lodging	6
Jamaica Rum pr Gallon proof	16,0
West India Ditto	14,0
Northward ditto	9,4
Brandy Proof	14,0
Whiskey ditto	9,4
Corn pr bushel	4,0
Clean Oats pr bushel	3,0
Oats in Sheaf pr Doz	1,0

Fodder ditto 1,0
Stablidge 6

Court then adjourned till court in Course, then to meet at the place appointed for the Public Buildings.

Test. M. Woods, Clk

John Patterson }
vs } Case
William Daniel } [16]

Settled.

Andrew Johnson Pickens }
vs } Case
John Trueman }

Judgment by default.

A. Jackson, Exe[r] }
S. Miers, deceased }
vs } Case
Julias Howard }
& James Tait }

Nonsuit.

John Oliver }
vs } Case
Henry Rose }

On Motion of M[r] Huntington, Attorney for the defendant, it is Ordered that dedimus potestatum do issue to Justices of the peace, for the county to take the examination of William Suit, of the State of North Carolina, according to interrogatories here in Court filed, and hereunto annexed.

Court adjourned untill Court in course.

M. Woods, Clk

At an Inferior Court, begun & held at Elbert Court House, the 17th day of April 1792.

Present, William Barnett, Even Ragland, Richardson Hunt, James Tait, esquires

---

Ordered that Francis Cook, Esquire be appointed Guardian of Martha Granger, on applicationof the said Martha, whereupon Joseph Moore came into court with said Cook, acknowledged themselves bound in the sum of five hundred pounds, for the faithful performance of said Cook as Guardian aforesaid.

Sam[l] Willison }
vs } Debt
Benj[a] Cook }

Benjamin Cook came in to court and confessed Judgment for nineteen pounds, eleven shillings, & Eleven pence, three farthings, with Cost of Suit, Stay of execution Sixty days.

John R. Ragland }
vs } Assumpsit
William Moss }

The defendant, by Nath[l] H. Churchill, his attorney, came into court and confessed Judgment, for six pounds specie, with Cost, with five months stay of execution.

Charles Goss, Security on the process.

Gidion Booker }
vs } Trespass
Thomas Carter }

Jury Sworn, to wit.

1.Francis Cook
2. Nathan Bonds
3. William Edwards
4. Sam[l] Tyner
5. John Burke
6. John Wilkins
7. George Russell
8. Thos. Penn
9. Jer[h] Wells
10. Daniel Madkins
11. John Dudley
12. Will Watkins

In the above case, it appearing that the Plaintiff had not used due diligence to have the Subscribing Witness, the Court ordered a nonsuit. [17]

William Allen }
vs } Debt
William Moss }

Judgment confessed for three hundred & fifty pounds, with Interest untill paid.

Test. W[m] Moss

Judgment Signed in open Court the Seventh day of April 1792.

Nath[l] H. Churchill, Atty for Plff

Thomas Walton }
vs } Debt
Benj[a] Ragland }

The Jury as in the case Gidion Booker vs Tho[s] Carter.

We the Jury find for the Plaintiff £41,19,4½ principal & Interest.

W[m] Watkins, F. M.

Joseph Davis entered himself Security in open Court.

Harry Kerr }
vs } debt
Mary Kerr }
vs }
John Turke & }
William Turk }

April Term 1792

The defendant came into Court, by Samuel Blackburn, his Atty, and confessed

---

Judgment for four pounds, ten shillings, Eight Pence, ½ penny, with five months stay of execution.

S. Blackburn, D. Atty

William Elliott }
vs } Cov[t]
Bradock McDonald }
& William Flanikin }

The same Jury as in the Case Booker vs Carter.

We the Jury find for the Plaintiff £13,19,5¼ Principal & interest.

William Watkins, F. M.

William Payton }
vs } Attachment
George Johnson }

The following Jury Sworn, to wit.

1. Peter Oliver
2. F. Cook
3. J. Hightower
4. H. McDonald
5. Thomas Scales
6. R. Martin
7. James Coleman
8. Wm Hightower
9. Benj. Ashworth
10. J. Dudley
11. Wm Guttery
12. J. Buckhanon

We the Jury find for the Plaintiff twenty eight pounds, five shillings, & Seven pence, & the Interest from date as Included in the above sum.

Hugh McDonald, F. M.

William J. Hobby } [18}
vs } Debt
Thomas C. Russell }

I confess Judgment for Eleven hundred and twenty pounds, with interest untill paid.

Test. Thomas C. Russell

J. Huntington

judgment Signed the Seventeenth day of April 1792.

N. H. Churchill, Atty for Plff

Satisfied 18th June 1793.

Joseph Nail }
vs } Case
Jesse Casey }
et al }

Jury Sworn, to wit.

1. Nathan Bonds	7. Thomas Russell
2. William Edwards	8. Jeremiah Wells
3. S. Tyner	9. D. Madkins
4. John Blake	10. William Watkins
5. John Wilkins	11. John Dudley
6. George Russell	12. James Carter

We the Jury find for the Plaintiff £87,S18,6.

Wm Watkins, F. M.

Ordered, that a Road be opened and cleared out the best and nearest way from Elbert Court House to the fish dam ford on broad River, & that Benjamin Baker, William Blake, & Francis Cook, be commissioners for Carrying

—

the same into effect, and that the Road be leading by Harts old Ferry be discontinued.

Ordered, that the order of the 20th of August last past, with Regard to Tavern Rates, be Resigned, & that the following order take place.

Ordered, that the following Rules be observed by persons who may obtain a licence for the present, to wit.

For Dinner	£0,1,6
Ditto Supper	1,2
Ditto breakfast	1,2
Lodging	6
Stableage	6
Corn & Oats p^{r} Gallon	6
Fodder p^{r} Bushel	1
Jamaica Rum p^{r} Gallon	16,0
Westindia Ditto	14,0
Northward Ditto	9,4
Brandy Ditto	14,0
Whiskey Ditto	9,4
Ginn Ditto	14,0
Cyder Ditto	2,4
Porter Ditto	9,4
Good Wine Ditto	14,0

A Petition from James Coleman & George Cook, by their attorney, Nath. H. Churchill, Esqr, praying to obtain licence to keep Taverns, In the Town of Petersburgh, the Court taking the same into consideration, whereupon

It is Ordered, that the said James Coleman & George Cook do obtain Licence for The Term [19} of one year, & from thence to the next Inferior Court, held for the said County, and no longer, upon giving Bond with approved Security, William Hatcher came into Court and offered himself Security, for the purposes above mentioned, who was approved of by the Court.

Middleton Woods presents a petition, praying Licence to keep a Tavern at Elbert Court House, The court taking the same into consideration, it is Ordered that the said Woods do obtain a Licence, by giving Bond as the Law directs. Thomas B. Scott & Robert Middleton came into Court and offered themselves Security, which was Excepted by the Court.

Court adjourned untill tomorrow 10 o'clock.

M. Woods

April 18th 1792

The Court Met agreeable to adjournment.

Present, William Barnett, Richd Hunt, Harry Caldwell, Esquires

---

Larkin Gatewood }
vs } Tresspass
James Carter }

Jury Sworn, to wit.

N^{o}	1. Nathan Bonds	7. Arch^{d} Smith
	2. John Buckhanon	8. Wm Edwards
	3. Wm Guttery	9. George Russell
	4. John Dudley	10. John Wilkins
	5. James Coleman	11. John Blake
	6. Thomas Cook	12. Saml Tyner

We the Jury find for the defendant.

James Coleman, Fore.

Elizabeth Rutherford }
by Benj[a] Rutherford }
her next friend }
vs } Slander
Edward McGarry }

Jury Sworn, to wit.

1. Archibald Burton
2. William Hatcher
3. George Cook
4. Thomas Napier
5. Robert Cosby
6. Thomas Penn
7. Jacob Whitworth
8. William Daniel
9. William Elliott
10. James Carter
11. A. McClary
12. A. Baker

We the Jury find for the Plaintiff fifty pounds, with Cost.

George Cook, F. M.

Barkley Martin }
vs } Case
William Carter }

The same Jury as in the Case Rutherford vs McGarry.

We find for the plaintiff £6,11,4¼.

W[m] Hatcher, F. M.

M[r] McGehee, Sect[y] in Court.

John Oliver } [21]
vs } Debt
Henry Rose }

The same Jury as in the case Gatewood vs Carter.

We find for the Plaintiff £8,8,8¼.

James Coleman, Fore.

Peter Martain acknowledged himself Security.

M. Woods.

Thomas Owen }
vs } Cov[t]
Daniel Stalker }
& Even Ragland }

Judgment confessed for twenty two pounds, six shillings, & four pence, & Cost of Suit, stay of Execution five months.

E. Ragland

Joseph Dobbs }
vs } Case
Charles Hutchings }

The same Jury as Rutherford vs McGarry.

We find for the Plaintiff £13,10,0.

W[m] Hatcher, F. M.

James Huling }
vs } Debt
William Carter }

Judgment confessed for the amount of Specialty, with interest, with five months stay, security being given as required by Law.

Mathews, Atty

Micajah McHee entered himself security.

M. Woods

Elijah Owens }
vs } debt
William Elliott }

The same Jury as in the Case Gatewood vs Carter.

We find for the Plaintiff £6,18,2.

G. Cook, Foreman

Hugh McDonald & John King Entered themselves Security.

William Smith }
vs } Case
Jacob Whitworth }

The defendant came into Court and confessed Judgment for the principal, interest, & Cost, with the Credits on the Note, with Eight months stay of execution, upon giving Security, the defendant is to pay upon the last Day of May two thousand weight of Tobacco, of Augusta Inspection, in part of said Judgment, at nine Shillings & four pence, this stay Granted only on the condition of the deft paying to Sam[l] Blackburn, atty for Smith, the said Tobacco upon the said day.

Jacob Whitworth

John Depriest acknowledged himself Security for stay of execution.

M. Woods

Moses Trimble }
vs } Case
John Luckey }

The same Jury as in the Case Rutherford vs McGarry.

We the Jury find for the Plaintiff £10,6,7¼.

W[m] Hatcher, Fore.

Thomas C. Russell } [22]
vs } Debt
Hugh McDonald & }
John Cunningham, esq[r] }

Judgment Confessed for the sum of twenty seven pounds, five shillings, & Eleven pence, with stay of execution untill the first day of January next, provided the defendant gives good and sufficient Security for the payment at that time, and upon giving such security, the said Thomas C. Russell is to deliver up a Bond, in possession held, as a Colateral Security, for the aforesaid Debt.

Blackburn, def[t] Atty

John King & E. McGarry entered themselves Security, app[d] by Court.

Nathan Bond }
vs } Case
Robert Martin }

Judgment confessed for ten pounds specie, with stay of Execution Six months.

Robert Martain

Peter Carnes }
vs } Case
William Moss }

The defendant came into Court and confessed Judgment for the sum of four pounds, thirteen shillings, & four pence, with Cost & five months stay of execution, an Security being given.

William Moss

I acknowledge myself Security for the above named William Moss, in the above Suit.

Charles Goss

The Court adjourned untill tomorrow 9 O'Clock.

April 19th, Court Met agreeable to adjournment.

Present, William Barnett, Even Ragland, Richardson Hunt, Harry Caldwell, Esqrs

Absolom Jackson }
vs } Case
William Carter }

Jury Sworn, to wit.

1. Thomas Cook
2. Archd Smith
3. Francis Cook
4. Robert Cosby
5. Nathl Bonds
6. John Depriest
7. William Daniel
8. William Hatcher
9. William Watkins
10. Moses Wilcox
11. James Banks
12. William Blake

We the Jury find for the Plaintiff £11,7,0.

William Hatcher, For.

Micajah Clark }
vs } Case
William Carter & }
Thos B. Scott }

The defendant came into Court and confessed Judgment, with interest, on five months stay of execution, Security being given, as required by Law.

Mr Meghee, Security. M. Woods

John Depriest } [23]
vs } debt
William Caster }

The defendant came into Court and confessed Judgment for the Specialty, with interest, on five months stay of execution, to Issue. J. White

M. McGee entered himself Security. John Mathews, Atty

Josias Jones }
vs } Trover & Conversion
Isaac Suttle }
Sarah, his Wife }
& William Moore }

The same Jury as in the Case Jackson vs Caster.

We the Jury find for the defendant.

Wm Watkins, F. M.

On Motion of Mr Walker, on behalf of Robert Middleton, Sheriff of the County of Elbert, Ordered, that a Protest be entered be entered in the words following, to Wit.

Elbert County } Robert Middleton, Sheriff of the County aforesaid, finding the Goal for the said County insufficient for the safe Custody for who may be confined by the direction of the laws of the Land, and fearfull of the ill consequences which may result from the escapes, is advised that it is necessary to Protest against the said Goal, and he doth most truly, Solemnly Protest against the same, as entirely insufficient for the safe Custody of persons.

Josias Jones }
vs } Trover & Con[v]
Sam[l] Blackburn }

Nonsuit.

Thomas P. Carnes }
vs } Case
John Depriest }
& John Crosby }

Dismissed at defendants Cost.

Ordered, that the following persons appointed Constables, for the Term of one year, and from thence to the next Succeeding Court, to Wit.

William Runnolds, Nathan Bond, Joseph Davis, Edward Goode, Stephen Haynes, John Dudley, Anthony Haney.

William Watkins }
vs } Cov[t]
Isham Thompson }
& Jim Thompson }

We the Jury find for the Plaintiff £7,0,8.

Walker Richardson acknowledges himself Security.

Test. M. Woods

Court then adjourned untill Court in Course.

Test. M. Woods W[m] Barnett, Evan Ragland, R. Hunt, Harry Caldwell

June 5th 1792. Elbert Court House [24]

Present, William Barnett, Richardson Hunt, Francis Cook, Esquires

The following persons were drawn as Jurors for the October Term (to Wit)

No
1. Julian Nail, Sen.
2. Francis Powers
3. John Spurs
4. Anthony Beverly
19. John Lowry
20. John Patterson
21. John Owens
22. Edward Walthall

5. William Lamb
6. Alexander Thompson
7. Thomas Woldridge
8. Wm Moon
9. Martin Tureman
10. Thomas Bucknold
11. Hugh McDonald
12. Isaac Morriss
13. Stephen Ramsey
14. Wm Spurs
15. Henry Parks
16. Ezekiel Wood
17. Howard Cash
18. Womack Blankinship

23. Thomas Webb
24. Peter David
25. Thomas Turin
26. Joseph Deadwelder
27. William Carter
28. William Allen
29. Thomas Wilkins
30. Robert C. Burton
31. Isaac Madows
32. John Reed
33. Edward Clarke
34. Moses Fleming
35. Sherod Harris
36. Elisha Miller

Middleton Woods, Clk

At an Inferior Court begun & held for the County of Elbert 16th day of October 1792.

Present, William Barnett, James Tait, & Even Ragland, Esquires

Phillip Colbertson came personally into Court and made choise of Thomas Colbertson, Senr as his Guardian, upon which Thomas Colbertson & Charles Goss & acknowledged themselves bound for the due performance of Thomas Colbertson, Senr, as Guardian of the above named Phillip Colbertson, under the penalty of five hundred pounds.

Patsey Colbertson came personally into Court and made choise of Charles Goss as her Guardian, upon which Thomas Colbertson, Senr & Thomas Colbertson, Junr & acknowledged themselves bound in the sum of five hundred pounds for the due performance of the said Charles Goss, as Guardian of the above named Patsey Colbertson, under the penalty of five hundred pounds.

Fanny Colbert came personally into Court and made choice of Thomas Colbert, Junr as her Guardian, upon which Thomas Colbertson, Senr & John Goss & acknowledged themselves bound for the due performance of the said Thomas Colbertson, Junr, as Guardian

of the above named Fanny Colbert, under the penalty of five hundred pounds. [25]

Nancy Colbertson, a minor, praying Guardian, the Court appointed Martha Madkins & James Madkin her Guardian, when William Daniel & John Patterson acknowledge themselves Securitys for the faithful discharge of their duties as Guardians for the above named Nancy, under the penalty of five hundred pounds.

Reuben Jourdon }
vs } Debt
James Dudley }

The defendant came into Court and confessed Judgment for the sum of Eleven pounds, eight & eight pence, to be discharged in Cows & Calves of the second quality, the said Cows not to be under three nor over six years old, at fifty Shillings each, on or before the fifteenth day of April next, and no execution to issue untill after the said fifteenth of April, other than for Cost.

James X Dudley his mark

Elizabeth Rutherford }
by Benj. Rutherford }
her next friend }
vs } Slander
Edward McGary }

The Court are of opinion that the Receipt produced, In this case, is a full Satisfaction for the Judgment of fifty pounds Recovered against the defendant, and do order Satisfaction accordingly to be entered up.

The Court then adjourned till tomorrow 10 O'Clock.

Attest. M. Woods

Wednesday 17th

Court Met pursuant to adjournment.

Present, William Barnett, James Tait & Evan Ragland, esquires

Thomas Carter }
vs }
Robert Martin }

Execution of fi fa issued in this case; and was levied, an affidavit was filed with the Sheriff, whereupon a Stay of Sale took place, and the Sheriff Reported the Case to this Court, the issue of fact made up between the parties was submitted to the following Jury.

1. Julian Nail
2. Thos Woldridge
3. Hugh McDonald
7. Edward Clarke
8. Joseph Deadwelder
9. Isaac Madows

4. Henry Parks	10. Moses Fleming
5. Howard Cash	11. John Darden
6. John Lowry	12. Edward Walthau

Who being impanneled and Sworn do say, We the Jury do find liable for Sale the Tract of Land, the Service of Squire, during the natural life of Robert Martin, also Letty, Harry, Fanny & Child.

Hugh McDonald

Caleb Fifer }
vs }
John King } [26]

Execution of fi fa issued in this Case, and was levied, an affidavit as filed with the Sheriff, whereupon a Stay of Sale took place, and the Sheriff Reported the case to the Court. Issue of fact made up Between the parties, it was Submitted to the following Jury, Viz.

1. John Buckhanon	7. Wamack Blankinship
2. Wm Booker	8. Francis Satterwhite
3. Thomas Cook	9. Alex. Thompson
4. James Coleman	10. William Akin
5. John Rogers	11. John Brown
6. Wm Brown	12. Thomas Crier

We being impaneled and Sworn, do say, We find the negroe liable for Sale.

Wm Booker, F. M.

Ordered, that Benjamin Ragland, William Watkins, & John Giles, with their hands, shall be Subject to work on the Road leading from Benjamins Raglands to Broad River.

The following persons were drawn as Jurors for the next Term, Viz.

1. Wm Gennings	8. Thomas Hilley
2. James Curtis	9. David Adams
3. Nathl Rositer	10. John Dobbs
4. Stephen Gardner	11. Jacob Myers
5. John Crosby	12. John Martin
6. Joseph Blackwater	13. William Wheeler
7. John Gill	14. William Cuningham
	15. John Patterson

16. Robert Armstrong
17. Joseph M. Russell
18. Wm Gordon
19. Wm Head
20. John Black
21. Drury Rose
22. Edward Crews
23. Voluntine Smith
24. Jacob Burton
25. Joshua Tiner
26. Abel Howell
27. Richard Bond
28. John Kees
29. James Walker
30. Jesse Rowell
31. James Brown
32. John Davis
33. Saml Meanes
34. Robert Ellice
35. John Muroney
36. Benj. Head

On Motion of Mr N. H. Churchill, Mary Garr came into court and prayed that Adam Garr Might be appointed Guardian, when William Head & Thomas Gregg acknowledged themselves bound in the sum of one thousand pounds for the due performance of Adam Garr, as Guardian for Mary Garr.

The Court proceeded to the choise of a Guardian for Sally Garr, Joel Garr, William Garr, Nancy Garr, Francis Garr, & George Garr, Minors, when Adam Garr was appointed, Thomas Gregg & Wm Head came into Court and acknowledged themselves bound in the sum of one thousand pounds, for the due performance of Adam Garr, as Guardian to the above named persons, who are minors.

Reuben Allen }
vs } Debt
Beverly Allen }

I do confess Judgment to Reuben Allen, in this case, for the sum of three thousand pounds against Beverly Allen, by his Special power, bearing date the first day of January 1791.

S. Blackburn, Deft Atty

Personally came into Court, Jane Brown and made choice of Elizabeth Cannon as her [27]
Guardian, upon which Thomas Scott, Esqr acknowledged himself Security for the performance of the said trust of Guardianship, under the penalty of one hundred pounds.

Ordered, that Thomas Scott, Esqr be considered Guardian for Patrick Brown, a Minor, whereupon Elizabeth Cannon came into Court and was accepted as Security for the performance of the said trust of Guardianship, under the penalty of one hundred pounds.

Ordered, that William Moss, esquire be appointed Guardian for Mary Stroud, Minor, whereupon Wamack Blankinship & Thomas Crier acknowledged themselves bound in the sum of one hundred pounds for the faithful performance of William Moss, Esq[r] as Guardian for the said Mary Stroud.

Ordered, that there be a Road opened and kept in Repair, from John Middletons on Savannah River to Elbert Court House, Crossing cold Water at Col[o] Cuninghams Mill, and that Joseph Henderson, W[m] Hansford, & Jacob Prewett, be & they are hereby appointed commissioners to carry the same into effect.

Court adjourned untill Court in Course.

William Barrett, James Tait, Even Ragland

At an Inferior Court, begun, held, and Continued at Elbert Court House, 2nd day of April 1793.

Present, William Barnett, James Tait, Evan Ragland, &Richardson Hunt, esquires

On the Petition of Sundry inhabitants of the County of Elbert, Ordered that, agreeable to said Petition, a ferry be established on the north fork of Broad River, at the Plantation of Jacob Odum, and a Road be laid out, from Elbert Court House, to said Ferry, and from thence to Hillhouses forge, that John Depriest, John Wingfield, & John Black be commissioners of said Road, from the Court House aforesaid to said Ferry, and that Cap[t] William Pattersn, James Crow, Nath[l] Smith, & Andrew Walker be commissioners of that part of the said Road, which leads from the said Ferry to the aforesaid forge.

William Moss }
vs }
Robert Burton }

Con[td] by the Plaintiff.

William Moss } [28]
vs }
John Patterson }

Continued by the Plaintiff.

W[m] Moss }
vs }
John F. Thompson }

Continued.

Robert Martin }
vs }
Benjamin Cook }

Settled.

On John Spurlock Setting forth that he is Blind and is not able to Support himself, Ordered that he Receive the sum of three pounds, to be provided for out of the moneys arising from the Sales of the Lotts in said County.

John Moore }
vs } Case
Charles Kennedy }

Dismissed.

Elijah Owens }
vs } Debt
Joseph M. Russell }

Settled, defendants Cost.

Court Adjourned till tomorrow 1 o'Clock.

Wednesday, 3rd day of April 1793.

Court Met pursuant to adjournment.

William Moss, administrator of the estate of Isham Stroud, deceased, this day applied for an order of Sale of the said estate.

On the Petition of Sundry inhabitants of said County, praying that a Road may be opened from McCunes Ferry, into the Road leading from Shockleys ferry, to the Iron Works, which is about Six miles in distance. Whereupon, it is ordered, that a Road be opened agreeable to said petition, and kept in repair, and that William McCune, Hugh King, and Richard Bond be and they are hereby appointed Commissioners, to carry the same into effect.

Beverly Greenwood }
by John Greenwood }
his Guardian }
vs } Slander
Harry Gatewood }

Jury Sworn, to Wit.

1. James Carter	7. John Blake
2. John Gill	8. Joshua Tyner
3. John Martin	9. Jesse Rowell
4. Jacob Myers	10. John Davis
5. William Wheeler	11. Samuel Meanes
6. William Head	12. Benj[a] Head

We the Jury find for the Plaintiff forty three pounds, fifteen shillings, and one penny, with Cost of Suit.

James Carter, Fore.

Joseph Hawthorn }
vs } Assault
Thomas Lovelady }
et al }

Settled, cost paid, M. W.

John Cobbs }
vs } Attachment
William Call }

M[r] Thomas Grier, a witness on the part of the plaintiff,

being old and infirm, On motion, it is ordered, that his testimony be taken in open Court, [29]
and Read as evidence, at the trial of the cause.

John Rogers }
vs } Debt
James Coleman }

The defendant came into Court and Confessed Judgment, for the sum of thirty seven pounds and nine pence, with interest till paid, and cost of suit, & ten months stay of execution, upon giving good Security.

James Coleman

James Tait entered himself Security for stay of Levy.

Jackson & Nightinggale }
vs } Debt
James H. Kidd }

In Virtue of a warrant of attorney, incorporated In the within mentioned bond, or obligation Given by the said James H. Kidd, to the said Amasa Jackson & Jon C. Nightingale, I do thereby, for the said James H. Kidd, & Confess Judgment against him for and to the use of the said Jackson & Nightingale for the sum of Sixty five pounds, four shillings, & five pence sterling, and Cost of Suit.

G. Walker, Atty def^t

Green & Co }
vs } Assumsit
Wm Carter }

Jury Sworn, to wit.

1. Rice Cleveland
2. Isham Thompson
3. James Allen
4. Joseph Terrell
5. Jesse Statham

---

6. John Rogers
7. James Coleman
8. John Buckhanon
9. Oliver White
10. Richard Easter
11. Garrald Walthall
12. Thomas Napier

We the Jury find for the plaintiff Seven pounds, Seven Shillings, & Eight pence, With Cost.

Isham Thompson, F. M.

Tommy Biggar }
vs } Debt
Charles Hudson }
& James Tait }

N. B., I Samuel Blackburn, attorney for Tommy Biggar, do agree that I will produce to the Within named obliges a bond given by Charles Hudson to Tommy Biggar, in the Room of which this bond, as and if that bond should be for Less than the sum mentioned in this bond, I will give Credit in this, Reducing this to the same.

Saml Blackburn

Agreeable to the above, I have produced the above mentioned bond, which is for the sum of fifty two pounds, fourteen Shillings, & Eight pence, which is the Real demand against the within obliges.

Samuel Blackburn, Atty
for Tommy Biggar

Have Reference to the process.

On the Petition of Elijah Brewer, praying to have a public Ferry established on broad [30] River, where Avington McLeroy formerly kept one, now the premises of your petitioner. Whereupon, it is ordered, that agreeable to said Petition, there be a ferry established at the usual place, said Brewer giving bond and Security, as the Law directs.

On application of John Braziel, Guardian for William Braziel, praying to have him bound unto John Cook, to learn the art and mistery of the black Smiths Trade.

Whereupon, it is ordered, that that the said William Braziel be bound unto the said Cook, for and during the term of five years, from and after the first day in March last past, said Cook giving bond as the Law directs in Such Cases.

On Information of James McCurdy, it is ordered, that Alexander Major be bound unto James McCurdy, untill he arrive to the age of twenty one Years, he giving bond and Security, to find him in Sufficient clothing, wholesome diet, and give him sufficient education.

When Stephen Groves with himself acknowledged themselves bound in the Sum of one Hundred pounds, to comply with the Law in such cases.

James McCurdy Stephen Groves

On Motion of M. Sullivan, Ordered, that Jacob Gilleyin obtain a Licence to keep a Tavern on the Road Leading to Petersburg, whereon he now lives, he giving Bond, as the Law directs, for and during the Term of one Year.

The Court adjourned untill tomorrow morning ten o'clock.

Thursday, 4th April 1793

The Court Met agreeable to adjournment.

Present, as Yesterday.

Walker Richardson }
vs } debt
William Flanekin }

Jury Sworn, to Wit.

1. John Black
2. John Gill
3. Abel Howell
4. Joshua Tiner
5. John Depriest
6. Oliver White
7. Absolom Baker
8. Dempsey Rogers
9. John Crowden
10. Benj[a] Head
11. John Davis
12. Ro. Cosby

We the Jury find for the Plaintiff £9,17,11.

John Davis, Fore.

Drury Thompson }
vs } Debt
John Cuningham }
& Wiley Davis }

Jury Sworn, to Wit.

1. Allen Daniel
2. Jno. Martin
3. James Cash
4. Thomas Cook
5. William Aycock
6. Henry Rose
7. Thomas Napier
8. Jn[o] Cook
9. Stephen Dedwelder
10. Sam[l] Meanes
11. Isham Thompson
12. Solomon Alston

We the Jurors find for the plaintiff £14,3,3¼.

Solomon Alston, Fore.

Isham Thompson } [31]
vs } Trespass vi et armus
Reuben Allen & }
Daniel Madkins }

Jury Sworn, to Wit.

1. Reuben Cook	7. William Aycock
2. Jn° Martin	8. Henry Rose
3. Solomon Alston	9. Thomas Napier
4. James Coleman	10. John Cook
5. James Carter	11. Christopher Dedwelder
6. Thomas Cook	12. Samuel Meanes

We the Jurors find for the defendants.

Solomon Alston, foreman

Jacob Bugg }
vs } Cov[t]
Abraham Colson }

James Tait, common Bail, came into court and acknowledged himself Special Bail.

Oliver White }
vs } Case
Henry Rose & }
John R. Ragland }

In this case, I confess Judgment for the defendant Henry Rose in the Sum of Eight pounds, Seventeen Shillings, & five pence, Specia, with a stay of execution till the first day of December next.

April 4th 1793

J. Huntington, Atty
for Henry Rose

William Kennedy & C° }
vs } Case
William Goode, Esq[r] }

James Coleman, common Bail, came into court and acknowledged Special Bail.

On a petition of a number of Inhabitants of said County, praying that there might be a Road, from Elbert Court House, to John Dudleys ford on Broad River, from thence along the dividing Ridge, between Little Choal Creek & Blue Stone, in the most direct way to Hillhouses furnace, and that Andrew McEver & John Fergus be appointed commissioners, to carry the Same into effect. Whereupon, it is ordered, that the prayer of the Petitioners be granted.

Thomas Brown }
vs } Assumpsit
Benj[a] Ragland }

The same Jury as in the Case of Walker Richardson vs William Flanekin, & Others.

The Came into Court and failing to answer, it was Considered a mistake.

William Allin }
vs } Debt
Henry Rose }

The defendant Came into Court and Confessed Judgment for the principal, Interest, & Cost untill paid.

Mathews, Atty for Def[t]

Henry Rose } [32]
vs } Case
Wamack Blankinship }
& Wiley Davis }

The defendant comes into Court and confessed Judgment for the Sum of Eleven pounds, Six Shillings, & ten pence. 4th April 1793

S. Blackburn, Atty
for defendant

Ordered, that the Rates to be taken by Tavern Keepers & Retailers of Spirituous Liquors be the Same as for the year 1792.

Absolom Baker }
vs }
the administrator }
of John Bowen, decd]

We the Jurors do find for the Plaintiff five hundred pounds, to be discharged on making Titles, agreeable to the condition of the said obligation.

James Coleman, foreman

William Allen }
vs } Case
Armstrong Heard }

Armstrong Heard came into Court and Confessed Judgment to William Allen for the sum of twelve pounds and five pence, half penny, with stay of execution five months, with interest & Cost.

Armstrong Heard

Test. Jno Griffin

William Allen }
vs } Case
James Head }

James Head came personally Into Court and confessed Judgment to William Allen for seven pounds, one Shilling, 4^{d}½, with Interest & Cost, with stay of execution five months.

April 4th 1793 James Head

Test. Jno Griffin

On a petition, ordered that a Road be opened from the furnace to William Daniels, from thence the most direct way towards Hatton ford, on Tugalo River, as far as Elbert line extends, and that Richard Ross & John McConnell be and they are hereby appointed Commissioners to carry the same into effect.

William Norris }
vs } Trespass ve et armes
Samuel Meanes }

Settled.

Florence Sullivan }
vs } Special Case
Hugh McDaniel }

Settled, def^{t} Cost.

Credit 17/6 to M. Woods.

Anthony Rowell }
vs } Case
Thomas Carter }

Dismissed.

McDowell & Thompson } [33]
vs }
Nattey Williams }

Dismissed.

Samuel Thompson }
vs } Case
Collin Reed }

Dismissed.

Thomas B. Scott }
vs } Case
John Davies }

Settled.

John Cuningham }
vs }
William Ward }

Settled. Blackburn to pay Cost.

John McDonald }
vs } Debt
Benjamin Ashworth }

Judgment Confessed.

James Meanes }
vs } Assault & Battery
Robert Stewart }

Settled.

Jesse White }
vs } Case
John Twedle }

Dismissed at the def[t] Cost.

David McCleskey }
vs }
John Leggett }

Settled, defendants Cost.

Benjamin Head }
vs } Case
Middleton Woods }

Settled.

—

Robert Martin }
vs } Case
William Chiselom }

Settled.

Lewis Geggett }
vs } Case
Lewis Hynor }

Settled.

On Motion, ordered, that John Baker do obtain A Licence to keep a Tavern, at the place where he now lives, he giving Bond, as the Law Directs in such Cases.

On Motion, ordered, that Absolom Baker do obtain A Licence to keep a Tavern, at Elbert Court House, on his own Lott, he giving Bond, as the Law Directs in such Cases.

The following persons was drawn to Serve as Jurors at the next Term, to wit.

1. John Cloud
2. Edward Ishman
3. Alexander King
4. David Vineyard
5. John Jones
6. Jonas Broach
7. James Hannah
8. Lunceford Kilgore
9. James Morrison
10. William Killett
14. John Thomason
15. William Tuggle
16. Brider Haney
17. Thomas Tait
18. William Cook
19. Joseph Akin
20. Eli Everson
21. Benj Goss
22. John Reed
23. John Lovingood

11. Stephen Williford
12. Benj. Porter
13. Noah Cloud

24. William Grimes
25. James Henderson
26. John Howrey
27. Amos Richardson

28. Benjamin Ragland
29. Christopher Dedwilder
30. Martain Dedwilder
31. James Currin

32. Joseph Bond [34]
33. Nathan Dabbs
34. John Terell
35.Ludford Parrott
36. John Clarkson

Henry Calton }
vs } Cov[t]
Hugh ~~McDonald~~ Sexon & }
H. Flanekin }

The defendant, by John Mathews, his attorney, Came into Court and Confessed Judgment for the sum of twelve pounds, ten Shillings.

Mathews, Atty

Court then adjourned untill Court in Course.

R. Hunt, James Tait, W[m] Barnett, Evan Ragland

At an Inferior Court, begun, held, and Continued at Elbert Court House, the first day of October 1793.

Present, W[m] Barnett, Even Ragland, R. Hunt, Esquires

Isham Thompson, appl }
vs } Appeal
George Cook, Resp[t] }

Jury Sworn, to Wit.

1. David Vineyard
2. Smith Cook
3. Jesse White
4. Dudley Cook
5. William Browner
6. Isaac Suttles

7. Jesse Statham
8. William Pulliam
9. Robert Burton
10. Joseph Akin
11. Christopher Dedwilder
12. W[m] Cook

Ordered, that the same be continued untill tomorrow.

Ordered, that Mr Thomas Scales be appointed Overseer over so much of the Road, leading by Mr Jonathan Arnolds, from Augusta to Franklin County ~~House~~, as he was formerly Commissioner of.

John Watkins }
vs }
John Depriest }

The same Jury as in the above Case.

We the Jury find for the Plaintiff 125,0,0.

Joseph Akin, F. M.

Ordered, That Thomas Burton & John Oliver be & they are hereby appointed Inspectors for Olivers Ware house, Mouth Broad River, for the year 1794, on their Giving Bond, with approved Security, & that James Tait, Esqr & Robert Thompson are hereby appointed to examine the Weights & Scales & Condition of the Ware House and Report thereof to the Inferior Court at the next Term.

Stephen Heard came into Court and acknowledged himself Special Bail for Hugh McDonald, [35] in the case of Michael & Sims against Hugh McDonald.

Hills & May }
vs } Ass^t
Wm Carter }

Jury Sworn, to Wit.

1. Thomas Cook	7. Joseph Blackwell
2. George Cook	8. Thomas Colbert
3. James Hannah	9. William Thomas
4. Christopher Moony	10. William Akin
5. Richard Bond	11. Jacob Whitworth
6. John Heard	12. Thomas Penn

We the Jury find for the Plaintiff £16,12,1, with Cost.

Geo. Cook, F. M.

On the Petition of a number of the Inhabitants of said County, praying that a Road be Opened from McCunes Ferry, on Savannah River, to William Higginbothams, Esqr, from the Beverdam

Creek, or near John Ferguses, from thence Crossing Broad River, at fork of Broad River, at or near John Ferguses, Esq[r], at Ewings Saw Mill, and that there be a ferry established at or near said Ferguses on Broad River.

The Court, Taking the same into consideration, Whereupon, it is Ordered, that the prayer of the petitioners be Granted, and that Jacob Higginbotham, Sam Young, and John Fergus be & they are hereby appointed Overseers of said Road.

William Allen }
vs } Case
Joseph Davis }

I, Joseph Davis, do hereby Confess Judgment to W[m] Allen, the Plaintiff, for the sum of Eleven pounds & two pence, with Interest & Costs, with Stay of execution Six months.

Joseph Davis

Test. John Griffin

On Motion of John Griffin, Ordered, that Benjamin Cook be authorized to dispose of Spirituous Liquors, and other, at the place where he now lives, upon his Complying with the Requisitions of the Law.

On Motion of M[r] J. Hobby, Ordered, that John Offutt be authorized to dispose of Spirituous Liquors, and other Liquors, in the Town of Petersburg, upon his Complying with the requisitions of the Law.

On a Petition of a number of Inhabitants of said County, praying that a Road may be Opened, from Elbert Court House, to Claibourn Webbs on Broad River, and that there be a ferry established on his Premises. Whereupon, it is ordered, that there be a Road opened from Elbert Court House, the most Direct & Best way to said Webbs, on boad River, and that Jesse White & John Webb Be & they are hereby appointed Commissioners

to carry the same into effect, and that Pleasant Webb & Absolom Baker be Overseers of [36]
the Same & also that there be a ferry established at said Webbs.

Court adjourned till tomorrow.

W. Barnett, Evan Ragland, Richarson Hunt

Wednesday, 2nd

The Court Met pursuant to adjournment.

Present, Wm Barnett, E. Ragland, R. Hunt, J. Taite, Esquires

Henry Rose, appl }
vs } Appeale
Wm Head, Rsp^t^ }

Settled at the appellants Cost.

Julias Howard }
vs } debt
John Rogers, Esqr }

I do confess Judgment in this case, for the principal, Interest, & Cost, with interest untill paid. October Term 1793

Test. John Rogers
S. Blackburn

Jesse White }
vs } Case
Wm Thomas & }
John Twedle }

William McCune, Esqr Came into Court and acknowledged himself Special Bail for Wm Thomas & John Twedle.

Wm Hatcher, appl }
vs } appeal
John R. Ragland, Rsp^t^ } for Justice Watkins

Jury Sworn, to Wit.

1. Wm Aycock	7. John Cook
2. Dudley Cook	8. Robert Pulliam
3. James Hannah	9. Joseph Cook
4. Isham Thompson	10. C. Moony
5. Wm Akin	11. George Cook
6. C. Dedwilder	12. [blank]

We find for the appellant, with Costs.

George Cook, F. M.

Avington McLeroy, appl }
vs } appeall
Thomas Walton, Rsp[t] }

Jury Sworn, to Wit.

1. Thomas Cook	7. W[m] Thompson
2. John Crowder	8. Thomas Carter
3. W[m] Aycock	9. W. H. Tait
4. W[m] Thomas	10. A. Walker
5. A. Whyte	11. G. Walthall
6. David Brown	12. James Camron

We the Jury find for Walton against McLeroy & Barnabas Pace the sum of £1,3,6.

Thomas Cook, F. M.

Thomas Gardner for } [37]
the use of Sam[l] Gardner }
vs }
Moses Rush, et all }

John Nelms & Robert Ellice came into Court and acknowledged themselves Special Bail for John Shields & Jeptha Rush, for Moses Rush.

John Cook, appl }
vs } appeall
W[m] Allen, Resp[t] }

Jury Sworn, to wit.

1. James Hannah	7. George Cook
2. W[m] Cook	8. Christopher Dedwilder
3. Isham Thompson	9. Robert Brown
4. W[m] Akin	10. Robert Pulliam
5. David Clark	11. Chris[t] Mooney
6. Benj[a] Ragland	12. W[m] Hatcher

We find for William Allen 10/2 ½.

George Cook, fore.

C[r] 9/4 p[r] J. Cook Ditto 9/4.

On Motion of Absolom Baker, Setting forth that, on or about the Commensement of the Present year, he petitioned for Licnce to keep a house of entertainment, and paid such money as was Required, and altho Such licence was Granted, he has found it inconvenient to enter into such Obligations, as the Law directs in Such Cases.

Ordered, that on the said Bakers paying such Costs We have accrued, that the Clerk of Elbert Court Replace the said Baker such moneys as he paid for such Licence.

William Moss }
vs }
John Paterson }

Settled, at the Plaintiffs Costs.

William Moss }
vs } Assump[t]
John F. Thompson }

Settled, at the Plaintiffs Cost.

Ro. Watkins }
vs } attachment
Drury Hutchins }

Settled.

Benj[a] Head }
vs } Cov[t]
Josiah Hamilton }

The same Jury as in the case of A. McLeroy vs Thomas Walton.

We the Jury find for the Plaintiff £100,0,0 and Interest & Cost.

Th[o] Cook, Fore.

Isham Thompson, appl }
vs } appeal
George Cook, Resp[t] }

Jury Sworn, to wit.

1. James Hannah	7. Ro. Brown
2. Wm Cook	8. C. Mooney
3. Wm Akin	9. W. Hatcher
4. David Clark	10. Josiah Cook
5. Ben^{j} Ragland	11. Dudley Cook
6. C. Dedwilder	12. Wm Daniel

We find for George Cook £2,15,3½.

Wm Booker, Sect^{y} stay of execution — Ben^{j} Ragland, Fore.

Claybourn Sandage, appl }
vs } Appeal
Robert Pulliam, Resp^{t} } [38]

The same Jury as In the Case of A. McLeroy vs Thomas Walton.

We the Jury find for Robert Pulliam 11/4, with Cost of Suit.

Th^{o} Cook, Forem.

Ro. Chambers }
vs }
Stephen Heard }

Settled, at the Plaintiffs Cost.

On a petition of James Isham, Minor, praying that Stephen Handley might be appointed Guardian for him, in lieu of Lofland Finnny, whereupon it is ordered that he be & he is hereby appointed Guardian.

Robert Ellice Came into Court and Acknowledged himself ~~Security~~ bound in the sum of fifty pounds for the faithfull performance of the said Handly as Guardian for said Isham.

Wm Allen }
vs
Andrew Johnson }

The Common Bail in this Case delivered up A. Johnson to the Court, Robert Ellice, Stephen Handly, & Thomas Burke, Senr came into Court and acknowledged themselves Special Bail.

Court adjourned until tomorrow Morning ten o'Clock.

Thursday, 3rd

Court Met agreeable to adjournment.

Present, William Barnett, E. Ragland, Richardson Hunt, Esquires

John Watkins }
vs }
John Depriest }

Judgment for £125,0,0.

The defendant came into Court and prayed an appeale, whereupon James Head & William Head came into open Court and acknowledged themselves Security for the appellant, that he Shall prosecute the appeal to Judgment, and that he shall pay the condemnation money or they will do it for him.

Thomas Brown }
vs }
Benja Ragland }

Jury Sworn (Viz.)

1. Archd Walker
2. James Hannah
3. Christopher Mooney
4. Wm Cook
5. Ro. Burton
6. John Wingfield
7. A. Johnson
8. John Crowder
9. Wm Burch
10. Wm Akin
11. Isaac Suttles
12. George Cook

We find for the Defendant.

George Cook, Fore.

Jacob Gillalin, appl } [39]
vs } Appeall
George Cook, Rspt }

Jury Sworn, Viz.

1. Thomas Cook
2. A. Whyte
3. R. Easter
4. Thomas Carter
7. Cristey Dedwilder
8. David Brown
9. James Camron
10. Dudley Cook

5. William Thompson
6. David Vineyard
11. Ben^j Ragland
12. Gilbert Barden

We the Jury find for George Cook 40/, with Cost of Suit.

Thomas Cook, Fore

James Hannah, Sect^y, stay of execution.

William Moss }
vs } Case
Robert Burton }

Settled, Plff Cost.

John Depriest }
vs } Case
Peter David }

Settled.

Henry Ross, appl }
vs } appeal
Wm Head, Resp^t }

Settled, Plff Cost.

Georgia, Elbert County }
October 4th 1793 }

We the administrators of the Estate of Michael Garr, Dec^d, the heirs of age, and Guardian of the Minors of said Estate do, in behalf of ourselves and Wards, Mutually agree that the Court shall chuse three discreet persons to appraise and divide the negroes belonging to the said Estate, and to sell the

—

Balance of the property, both real and personal, of the estate to the highest bidder, at twelve months Credit, after giving two months Notice by advertisement at the Court House of Elbert County, the amount of which balance shall be equally divided betwixt the heirs now of age and the Minors of said Estate, the shares of Minors to be put into the hands of their Respective Guardian, for which they are to be accountable, and do Mutually agree to make this agreement the order of the Court, and that any debt which may be Oweing by the estate are first to be paid, each Claiment containing his equal share either by himself or Guardian.

Test. Saml Blackburn   Lewis Garr, Adam Garr, James Brown

Ordered, that the above petition be Granted, & that Thomas B. Scott, Ralph Banks, & Joseph Henderson be and they are hereby appointed to appraise and divide the above mentioned negroes, and to sell the within named Balance of said Estate, agreeable to the within petition.

On a petition of Thomas Carter, praying that a Ferry may be established about 3 or 4 hundred yards above the mouth of Deep creek, and about four miles above Dudley's ferry.

Ordered, that the above petition

be Granted, on Thomas Carters Complying with the Requisition of the Law. [40]

On a petition of John Sweze, praying that Robert Kennedy may be appointed Guardian for him. Whereupon, it is Ordered, that the prayer of the petitioner be granted. Wm Johnson Came into Court and acknowledged himself Security, in the sum of fifty pounds, for the faithfull performance of the said Kennedy, as Guardian as Guardian for John Sweze.

On the petition of James Coleman, by William J. Hobby, his attorney, praying that he might Renew his Tavern Licence. Whereupon, it is Ordered, that the prayer be granted, on his complying with the Requisition of the Law.

Thomas Brown }
vs } Judgment for the defendant
Benjamin Ragland}

The plaintiff prayed an appeal, Joseph Blackwell acknowledged himself Security for the prosecution of the appeal.

M. Woods

To the Justices of the Inferior Court for the County of Elbert

The petition of James Alston, Respectfully Sheweth that he has become the perchaser of a tract of Land on Savannah River, formerly the property of Henry Hunt, and once in dispute between

said Hunt and Alexander McAlphin, Dec^{d}, and decided on by Rule of reference in the County of Wilkes, before the division of the said County, and as the said lands are now in the County of Elbert, the defendant deceased, and no division of the said Land taken place, your petitioner therefore prays that the said Land may be divided by persons appointed by the Court, agreeable to the award to the said Arbitrators, which is hereunto annexed, and your petitioner will pray &c.

Walker, Atty for Alston

On the petition of James Alston, Ordered, that John Darden & Robert Middleton do attend the County Surveyor, Richardson Hunt, Esqr, who is appointed to lay off and divide the said Land according to the tenor and effect of the said Award and Judgment of Wilkes Court.

Amos Ponder }
vs }
John Depriest & }
James McCleskey }

Settled at the Plaintiffs Cost.

Court adjourned untill Court in Course.

Wm Barnett, R. Hunt, Evan Ragland

February 28th 1794 [41]

The following persons was drawn to serve on the Jury at the next Term, to wit.

1. Benjamin Allen
2. James Collins
3. Benj^{a} Cook
4. Laughlin Fanin
5. Josiah Hopkins
6. Thomas Colbert, Senr
7. James Brown
8. Joshua Tinor
9. Harmon Lovingood
10. Pleasant Webb
11. Thomas Ewing
12. Arthur Jones
13. Anthony Beverly
14. Christopher Starr
15. Josiah Certain
16. Stephen Stephens
17. Joel Butler
18. Brown Dye
19. James Brown
20. Thomas Head
21. James Lowry
22. John Glover
23. Wm Garham
24. Nicholas Sewell
25. Isaac Meadows
26. Eliab Vinson
27. Wm Brawner
28. Nathan Bonds
29. John Johnson
30. John Brown
31. John Cooper
32. John Black
33. Joseph King
34. William Tweedle
35. Joshua Cook
36. Benj^{a} Merritt

At an Inferior Court, begun, held, and Continued for Elbert County 1st day of April 1794.

Present, Wm Barnett, E. Ragland, Richardson Hunt, James Tait, Esquires

---

On Application of Minor Marsh, Ordered, that he be exempted from paying his poll Tax for the year 1793.

Ralph Banks }
vs } debt
Benj[a] Head & }
Adam Gaar }

I do hereby Confess Judgment for the sum of eleven pounds, five Shillings, & Seven pence, to the within named Ralph Banks.

Adam Garr

Benj[a] Cook, Josiah Certain, Thomas Head, Anthony Beverly is exempted from Serving on the Jury, for the present Term.

Ordered, that William Runnolds be appointed Constable for the district of Petersburg.

Lucy & Nancy Adams Came into Court and Made choise of Archer Burton as their Guardian, the Court proceeded to appoint a Guardian for Sally, Henry, & William Adams, Minors, when Archibald Burton was appointed, whereupon Peter Oliver came into Court and acknowledged himself bound in the sum of one thousand five hundred pounds, for the faithfull performance as Guardian for the persons above named.

Ordered, that Elisha Brewer be appointed a Guardian for Edmond Brewer, minor, Robert L. Tait Came into Court and acknowledged himself bound in the sum of one

Hundred and fifty pounds for the faithfull performance as Guardian for Edmond Brewer, [42]
Minor.

John Chiseholm }
vs } Case
Robert Selfridge }

The following Jury Sworn, to wit.

1. John Carson
2. Benj[a] Brown
3. Lewis Mosely
4. Daniel Casey
5. L. Fanin
6. Joshua Tiner
7. Thomas Owing
8. Pleasant Webb
9. James Brown
10. W[m] Graham
11. W[m] Brawner
12. Joshua Cook
13. John Brown

We the Jury find for the Plaintiff £23,18,0.

Joshua Carson, forem.

appeal.

Phillip Conaway}
vs }
Bazil Herman }

Jury Sworn, to wit.

1. Thompson McGuire	7. Wm Guttery
2. Robert Selfridge	8. Giptha Riesh
3. Robert Hudleston	9. Amas Richardson
4. Garrad Walthall	10. Mathias Ward
5. John Shields	11. William Ward
6. Jesse White	12. Robert Shepperd

We the Jury find for the Plaintiff sixteen pounds, with Cost.

Gerrold Walthall, Fore.

William Moon came into Court & acknowledged himself Security on the above Suit for the stay of execution according to Law.

Edward Moore }
vs }
William Daniel }
& David Woodson }

Continued by consent.

Ordered, that William Cunningham be appointed overseer of the Road leading through Capt Pattens Militia Company, from high shoals on Broad River, to Hillhouses Furnace, and Capt Hodge overseer on said Road leading through his own Company, and Captain Heard in his own Company.

Ordered, that Nehemiah Howard, Ralph ~~Banks~~ Owens, and Moses Hughes be and they are hereby appointed Inspectors of Tobacco at Lightwood Logg Ware house, on the County of Elbert, they giving bond and Security, and taking the Oath by Law prescribed.

Elijah Owens and Middleton Woods acknowledged themselves Bound as Security for the faithfull performance of the above mentioned Persons as Inspectors, at said Warehouse according to Law.

Ordered, that Benjamin Cook be appointed overseer over that part of the Road, leading from McKleroy's Ferry, to Elbert Court House, as far as the Shool house, and John Hubberd from thence to Francis Cook's, Esqr.

The Court adjourned till tomorrow ten o'Clock.

Wednesday, 2nd April 1794 [43]

The Court met pursuant to adjournment.

Present, William Barnett, James Tait, Richardson Hunt, & Saml Higgenbotham, Esquires

Harry Caldwell }
vs } Case
Gerrald Walthall}

Jury Sworn, to wit.

1. Benjamin Brown	7. John Shields
2. Daniel Casey	8. Jesse White
3. Laughlin Fannin	9. Stephen Rush
4. Thomas Ewing	10. Mathias Ward
5. Pleasant Webb	11. William Ward
6. Wm Graham	12. Thompson McGuire

We the Jury find the defendant requited.

Thompson McGuire, Fore.

Ordered, that James Ware be appointed Commissioner in lieu of Andrew McEver, who neglects to serve on the Road, leading from Elbert Court house, to Dudley's ford on Broad River, thence to Hillhouses furnace, to act in Conjunction with John Rogers.

Jesse White }
vs } Case
William Thomas}
& John Tweedle }

I, William Thomas, do confess Judgment, in this case, for the Sum of Eight pounds, fifteen Shillings, with Interest till paid, and cost of Suit, with Six months Stay of Execution, upon giving Security, according to Law.

John Clarkson acknowledged }
himself Security. }

William Thomas

G. Crump }
vs }
William Goode }

Jury Sworn (to wit)

1. John Brown
2. Robert Canada
3. ~~John~~ Wm Brown
4. John Cason
5. John Henderson
6. E. Harbour
7. Thomas Cook
8. Luke Hambleton
9. James Coleman
10. John Oliver
11. Leroy Pope
12. Robt Thompson

We the Jury do find for the plaintiff forty one pounds, nineteen Shillings, & ten pence.

Leroy Pope

David Hillhouse }
vs } Debt
Wm Chisolm }

The same Jury as in the case Harry ~~Caldwell~~ Walthall.

We the Jury find for the plaintiff Sixty one pounds, two Shillings, and Eight pence, with Cost.

Thompson McGuire, For.

Thomas C. Russell }
vs } Case
Gerrald Walthall }

I confess a Judgment on the within for the Sum of thirteen pounds, Eighteen Shillings, and four pence, with a Stay of Execution till the Second day of April 1795.

Gerrald Walthall, Junr

Abraham Colson }
for Culberd Hudson }
vs } Debt
James Coleman }

[44]

I confess Judgment on the within for the Sum of one Hundred & 49 pounds, Eleven Shillings, with Stay of Execution untill the twenty fifth December 1794, with Interest, and Cost of Suit.

James Coleman, For.

James Alston }
vs }
Abner, otherwise }
called, Abb McKlee }

I do Confess Judgment, in this Case, in behalf of Avington McKleroy, and by his particular Instruction, for the Sum of Sixteen Pounds Specie, with Interest till paid, and five months Stay of Execution.

Blackburn, Def[t]

Benjamin Harris }
vs } Case
Thomas Carter }

I do hereby confess Judgment to Benjamin Harris, ass[ee] of Thomas Glascock, for the Sum of five pounds, with Interest, and Cost of Suit, with Stay of Execution five Months.

Court then Adjourned untill tomorrow to ten o'Clock.

Thursday, 3rd April 1794

Court met Pursuant to Adjournment.

Present, William Barnett, James Tait, Evan Ragland, Samuel Higgenbotham, Esquire's

E. Gillium }
vs } debt
Exe[rs] James Meredith }

Jury Sworn (to wit)

1. William Browner	7. John Lowry
2. Pleasant Webb	8. William Dodd
3. Burket Green	9. John Depriest
4. John Dawsey	10. William Daniel
5. John Brown	11. Hugh McDonald
6. James Flood	12. A. Millian

We the Jury do find for the defendant.

And, Robert Cosby acknowledged }
himself Security for an appeal. }

H. McDonald, Fore.

John Whitney }
vs }
William Elliott }

Jury Sworn (to wit)

1. Henry Cook	7. Benjamin Ashworth
2. Isaac Settle	8. Walker Richardson
3. E. Harbour	9. William Moore
4. John Jones	10. James Head
5. Robert Ellis	11. John Wingfield
6. Stephen Fulgem	12. William Cunningham

We the Jury find for the plaintiff £6,9,1½.

E. Harbour

Charles Hutchings } [45]
vs } Attachment
Samuel Hunter }

Settled.

Nancy Stephens }
vs }
Benjamin Ragland }

Jury Sworn (to with)

1. William McCune	7. William Allen
2. Oliver White	8. John Henderson

3. Samuel Nelson
4. Laughlin Fannin
5. John McConnell
6. Wiley Davis
9. Thomas Hanie
10. Tho. B. Scott
11. Leroy Pope
12. A. Baker

We the Jury find for the plaintiff Eighty nine pounds, three Shillings, and three pence.

Leroy Pope

James Little & }
Robert McAlpin }
vs } Debt
Jacob Whitworth }
& Armstrong Heard }

Nonsuit.

William Allen }
vs }
David McCleskey }

Settled.

Ordered, that William Adams be ~~appointed~~ bound unto Lewis Mosely, he complying with the terms of the

William Allen }
vs } Case
Benjamin Head }

The same Jury as in the case Whitney vs Elliott.

We the Jury find for the ~~defendant~~ Plaintiff forty five pounds, Seventeen Shillings, & Six pence, half penny.

E. Harbour, Foreman

William Allen }
vs } Case
Laughlin Fannin }

I do hereby confess Judgment, for the within Sum of Eight Pounds, five Shillings, and ~~Eight~~ & three pence, with Interest, and Cost of Suit.

April 3rd 1794 John C. Walker, Att^y for Def^t

James Gaines }
vs } Special Case
Joseph Blackwell }

Nonsuit.

Joseph Staton, acting Executor }
of John Heard, Senr, Dec^d }
vs } Debt
Stephen Heard, Esqr }

The same Jury as in the Case Gillum vs Meredith.

We the Jury find for the Plaintiff the Sum of thirty Pounds.

Hugh McDonald, Fore.

David Brown & }
James Camron }
vs } Case
James Cook }

Jury Sworn, to wit.

1. Leroy Pope
2. James Little
3. E. Harbour
4. Benjamin Ashworth
5. William Moon
6. John Wingfield
7. William Cunningham
8. Samuel Nelson
9. L. Fannin
10. John McConnell
11. John Henderson
12. Thomas Hanie

We the Jury find for the Plaintiff on Hundred Pounds Damages.

Leroy Pope

The Court then adjourned till tomorrow.

Friday, 4th April 1794 [46]

Court met Pursuant Adjournment.

Present, as Yesterday

Leroy Pope }
vs }
Ben^{j} Head }

Wiley Davis, being Summoned, a Garnishee in the above cause, Sayeth he has np property in his possession, not had any at the time of Being so Summoned, except a Bond on David McCleskey for £200 to make rights to 430 Acres of Land in the County of Franklin, tho is not certain that the Bond is the property of Benjamin Head, but the Plaintiff Suggesting that that there were in his possession (to wit}

200 Acres of Land and four Negroes, now in the possession of the same, by attachmt. the Court are of Opinion that the whole of the proceedings Stand over untill next term.

Saml Watkins }
vs }
Benjn Head }

Wilie Davis, being duly Summoned, as Garnishee in the above case, Sayeth he hath no property in his possession, except a bond on David McCleskey for £200 to make ~~titles~~ Rights to 430 Acres of Land in the County of Franklin, tho is not certain that the Bond is the property of right to Benjamin Head, but the plaintiff Suggesting that there were property in his possession, to wit. 200 Acres of Land and four Negroes, now in his possession of the same

---

Law by attachment. The Court are of Opinion that the whole of the proceedings Stand over untill next term.

William Strong }
vs } Case
John Depriest }

Settled, at the defendants cost.

William Graham}
vs } Case
John Depriest }

I do confess Judgment for the Sum of Eleven pounds, ten Shillings, and four pence, with Interest till paid, and Cost of Suit, to be Stayed agreeable to Law, on Security being given.

Blackburn, Def^{t} Att^{y}

Tho. C. Russell }
vs } debt
John Thompson }

Jury Sworn, to wit.

1. Wm Chisolm	7. John Heard
2. Saml King	8. Andrew Millioun
3. Rid Coulter	9. Wm Grimes
4. Charles Coulter	10. Rid Colbert
5. James Camron	11. James Head
6. Wm Moore	12. Pleasant Webb
	13. Oliver White

We the Jury find for the Plaintiff Seven pounds, three, & Six pence, with Interest, and Cost of Suit. Benjamin Cook acknowledged himself Secty.

Saml King, Foren

J. Allison }
vs }
Geo. Darden }

Jury Sworn (to wit)

1. John Brown	7. Wm Cunningham
2. Isaac Settle	8. Saml Nelson
3. William Oliver	9. L. Fannin
4. Benjamin Ashworth	10. John McConnell
5. Wm Moore	11. John Henderson
6. John Wingfield	12. Thomas Hanie

We the Jury find for the plaintiff the sum of fourteen pounds, with Cost of Suit.

Wm Oliver, Foren

David Watkins } [no page number]
for the use of }
Henry Giles }
vs } Debt
William Daniel }

The same Jury as in The case Brown & Camron vs Cook.

We the Jury do find for the defendant.

Leroy Pope, Fore.

James Cook for }
Leroy Pope }
vs } Case
James Camron & }
David Brown }

We do confess Judgment in this Case, for the sum of twenty one Pounds, with Interest till paid, upon giving Security Agreeable to Law, with Seven Months Stay of Execution.

Benjamin Cook came }
into Court and acknow }
ledged himself Sc^{y} }

James Camron
David Brown

Robert Tait, for the }
use of Morgan Richardson }
vs } Cov^{t}
Wm Carter }

Nonsuit.

Leroy Pope }
vs } Cov^{t}
Jacob Whitworth }
and Saml Winbish }

Settled, at the Defendants cost.

Michael & Sims }
vs } Cov^{t}
Hugh McDonald}

I do hereby Confess Judgement to Michael and Sims for the Sum of five pounds, Eleven Shillings, & nine pence, half penny, with Interest and Cost of Suit, and Stay of Execution till 25th Decem^{r} next.

John Griffin

Hugh McDonald

John Follett }
vs } Debt
Wm Higgenbotham }

The same Jury as in the Case of Brown & Camron vs Cook. We the Jury find for the Plaintiff one Hundred and fifteen pounds, ten Shillings.

John McConnell, For^n

Saml Higgenbotham }
came into Court and ack }
nowledged himself Sec^y }

James Depriest for the use }
of James Cunningham }
vs } Case
William Moon }

I do confess Judgment for the Sum of Six Pounds Sterling and Cost of Suit, with Stay of Execution till 25th December next.

William Moon

Alexander Thompson }
vs }
John Davis }

Settled, at the Def^t Cost.

John Tweedle } [47]
vs }
John Fleetwood }

Dismissed.

Robert Martin }
vs } attachment
Edmond Graves }

Jury Sworn, to wit.

1. Hugh McDonald
2. Peter Whale
3. Thomas Cook
4. Stephen Rush

7. James Camron
8. David Brown
9. Wm Graham
10. Richard Colbert

5. John Heard | 11. Samuel King
6. W[m] Moon | 12. W[m] Daniel

We the Jury find for the plaintiff the Sum of fifty pounds, with Lawfull Interest, Since due, and cost of Suit.

Hugh McDonald

John Depriest }
vs } att[t]
Thomas Martin }

Jury Sworn (to wit)

1. Benj[n] Brown
2. W[m] Chisolm
3. Andrew Millicun
4. Ch[s] Coulter
5. John Cook
6. Tho[s] Coper
7. John McCever
8. Peter Martin
9. Ric[d] Gatewood
10. Ric[d] Coulter
11. Alex Hunter
12. Randolph Holbrooks

We the Jury find for the plaintiff forty Pounds, with Interest and Cost of Suit.

A. Millicun, Foreman

James Cook }
vs }
Joshua Stead}

Dismissed.

Nath[l] Durkee }
vs } Debt
James Stewart }

The same Jury as in the case Martin & Graves.

We the Jury find for the plaintiff, the Sum of twelve pounds, Eighteen Shillings, with Lawfull Interest, Since the first of January 1791, with Cost of Suit.

Hugh McDonald, For[e]

—

John Boyd }
vs } Trespass
Benjn Ashworth }

The same Jury as in the case Martin & Graves.

We the Jury find for the Plaintiff the Sum of fourteen pounds, five Shillings, and ten pence, with Cost of Suit.

Richard Coulter }
vs } Case
John Depriest }

Settled, at the Defendants Cost.

William Kennedy & Co }
vs } Case
William Goode }

Nonsuit.

Commissioners }
vs }
Joseph Blackwell }

Settled.

Court adjourned till tomorrow 10 O'clock.

Saturday, 5th April 1794

The Court met Pursuant to adjournment.

Present, as Yesterday

Ordered, that Nathaniel Hudson be and he is hereby appointed Overseer over that part of the Road, that leads from Petersburgh to Elbert Court house, (to wit) from the part of the Road at Wm Thompsons, to the Cross Road at Francis Cook, Esqr. And, John Upshaw from Cooks to Tuttle Shoal, on the Beaverdam. And, James Shields from Tuttles to the Morur. And, Peter Tidwell from thence to the Franklin line.

Ordered, that Luke Hambleton be appointed Overseer over that part of the Road leading from McCunes Ferry to Elbert Court House, as farr as Teasley Mill on Cold Water. And, John

Teasly from thence to Wm Hammonds and Wm Howards, from thence to the Court House. [48]

Ordered, that Nathan Bonds be appointed Overseer over the Road from Brewers Ferry, on Broad River, to the Cherokee ford on Savannah River.

Ordered, that William Watkins be appointed Overseer of the Road from Petersburgh to Coodys Creek. And, Stephen Ellington from thence to Buttroms Creek. And, M. J. Williams from thence to Warhatchee. And, Christopher Clark, Junr from thence to the fish Dam. And, Charles Goss from thence to Ceder Creek. And, Jonas Brock from thence to White Mill. And, Wm Dudley Deep Creek ~~and William Dudley~~ from thence to the County line, John Furgus.

Ordered, that James Hoof be the Overseer of the Road from Elbert Court House to Mrs Mitchells, and John Blake from thence to the Fish Dam ford.

Ordered, that Wm Haley be appointed Overseer of the Road from the fork this side of Petersburgh, up the Same to Cross path Opejct to William Winn and Samuel McGeehee, from thence to William Allens, and William Arnold, from thence to Vanns Creek, and John Rucker from thence to Cunninghams, and thence to Arnold Store, H. Bailey, and from thence to Lightwood Thomas Scales is hereby appointed.

Ordered, that Amos Richardson be appointed Overseer over that part of the Road from Shockley Ferry to John Fergus, as far as bigg Ceder Creek.

And, James McDonald from thence to James Shields, And from thence to John Fergus Mill, B. Price is appointed. And, from thence to Ewings Mill, James Cowden is appointed.

John Depriest is hereby appointed Overseer from Elbert Court House to Odems Ferry, and Saml Woods from thence to Mr Hodges, and Francis Hodges, from thence to the forge.

Ordered, that Thomas Carter & Thomas Burk be appointed Commissioners from McGowens Ferry to Dudleys Ferry, thence towards the Cherokee Corner.

From Shockleys Ferry to Wm Dudleys, Peter Brown and John Ross be and they are hereby appointed Commissioners from the Court House to [illegible] McKeana & Ja^{s} Reyles be and they are hereby appointed Commissioners.

John McEver }
vs }
Richd Coulter }

Settled.

Jacob Bugg }
vs }
Abraham Colson }

Settled.

C. Crikutt }
vs }
Absalom Baker }

Settled.

Ric[d] Coulter }
vs }
Rob[t] Smith }

Settled.

W[m] Norris }
vs }
W[m] Ward }

Settled.

Abraham Colson }
vs }
Jacob Bugg }

Settled.

Drury Thompson } [49]
vs }
Peter Ragsdale }

Settled.

William Dudley }
vs }
John Starr }

Settled.

The Court then adjourned till Court in Course.

William Barnett, James Tait, R. Hunt, Saml Higginbotham

The following Persons were Drawn to Serve on the Jury at the next term, (to wit)

1. John Boyd
2. Elias Hendrick
3. Ezekiel Wells
4. Mark Duncan
5. John Smith
6. John Shakleford
7. Thomas Guttery
8. Joseph McClary
9. John McKee
10. Oliver Rock
11. John Albrittin
12. Robert Ellis
13. John Kilgore
14. Isham Morgan
15. John Patterson
16. Wm Duff
17. Edmond Rowsy
18. John Pollard
19. Thomas Pinnian
20. John Brown
21. Andrew Millicun
22. Thomas King
23. Nathan Alexander
24. Zachariah Thomas
25. Luke Hambleton
26. Whitfields Bond
27. John Scales
28. Wm Johnson
29. Saml King
30. Robt C. Burton
31. Isaac Morris
32. Wm Edwards
33. Demsey Rogers
34. Benjamin Davis
35. Moses Hill
36. James Brown

R. Hunt

At an Inferior Court, begun, held, and Continued the 30th day of September 1794.

Present, William Barnett, James Tait, Evan Ragland, R. Hunt

John Cobbs }
vs } Att^{t}
William Call }

Jury Sworn (to wit)

1. Elias Hendricks
2. Ezekiel Wells
3. John McKee
4. Oliver Rock
5. Robert Ellis
6. Isham Morgan
7. Edward Rowsy
8. Demsy Rogers
9. Andrew Millicun
10. Luke Hambleton
11. William Johnson
12. Saml King

We the Jury find for the Plaintiff Three Hundred and ninety nine pounds & one penny.

A. Millican, F. M.

Henry Smerdon
vs }
David McCleskey }

Jury Sworn (to wit)

1. Wm Hatcher	7. Thomas Burton
2. Drury Thompson	8. D. McDonald
3. Robert L. Tait	9. John Carrell
4. E. Brewer	10. John King
5. Thomas Napier	11. William Burch
6. Thomas Cook	12. Booker Easter

We the Jury find for the Plaintiff five pounds, nine Shillings, and four pence, with Lawfull Interest.

Wm Hatcher, Fore^mn^

James Brewer, Minor, Came into Court, and petitioned that Robert L. Tait might be appointed his Guardian. Whereupon, it is Ordered, that be and he is hereby appointed, he giving bond with Sec^ty^ in the Sum of two Hundred pounds for his faithfull performance as such. Isham Thompson and Richmond Cosby came into Court and acknowledged themselves Sec^ty^ in terms of the Law.

Isaac Jones }
vs }
Isaias Harbour }

The Same Jury as in the case Smerdon vs McCleskey.

We the Jury find for the Plaintiff twenty five pounds, with Cost.

Wm Hatcher

On Motion of Wm Runnolds, Ordered, that he Obtain a Licence to keep a tavern in [50] Petersburgh,he Complying with the Requisits of the Law. Isham Morgan Came into Court & Acknowledged himself Se^ty^ in the Sum of fifty pounds for the Complyance of the said Runnold in Keeping a public house in Petersburh, According to Law.

Horatio Gates Brewer, Minor, came into Court and prayed that William Brewer might be appointed his Guardian. Whereupon, it is Ordered, that he be appointed on his Complying with the requisits of the Law. Lemuel Black and Robert Cosby came into Court and acknowledged themselves bound in the sum of Two Hundred pounds for the faithfull performance of said Brewer as Guardian as above.

On petition of a number of Inhabitance of the upper End of Elbert County, praying that a Road might be opened from the said part to the Court House.

Whereupon, is Ordered, that Joseph Nail, Rich[d] Tyner, and Donald McDonald be and they are hereby appointed Commissioners to Carry the Same into effect.

On the petition of the Inhabitance of Elbert County, praying that the Road be turned by the New Inspetion which now Crosses the Creek some Distance Above.

Ordered, that there be a publick ferry at the Mouth of Lightwood Logg on Elijah Owens premises. Court adjourned, tomorrow, &c.

Wednesady, 1st October 1794

Present, William Barnett, James Tait, Evan Ragland, R. Hunt, S. Higginbotham

Benjamin Thurman }
vs }
Leroy Pope }

Jury Sworn (to wit)

1. Elias Hendricks	7. John Boyd
2. John McKee	8. William Johnson
3. Isham Morgan	9. Sam[l] King
4. Andrew Millicun	10. Jeptha Rush
5. William Edwards	11. W[m] Hatcher
6. Walker Richardson	12. W[m] Booker

We the Jury find for the Plaintiff forty nine pounds 2/1.

W[m] J. Hobby acknowledged himself Se[ty] } W[m] Hatcher, For[n]
for Stay of Levy }

Commissioners }
vs }
Benj. Baker }

I do confess Judgment in this case, for the principal, Interest, and cost, with Interest ~~and Cost~~ till paid, and Stay of Execution, till the first day of January next.

Test. Sam[l] Blackburn — Benj. Baker

James Ponder }
vs }
W. Richardson }

I do Confess Judgment in this case for the principal Contained in the Note Served up with Interest and Cost till paid.

W. Richardson

Sam[l] Blackbourn

Ric[d] Colbert }
vs }
Perry Head }

Peron Pharrow, Summoned as Garnishee, declared that at the time he was Served with a Copy Writ, he had Sold a tract of Land to B. Head, containing 400 acres on Vanns Creek, & had not Conveyed tittles to the Same at that time. Paron Farrow further Saith that Wiley Davis came over into South Carolina, and

asked him for tittles, which he refused to make, as he did not think he was Safe, and said [51] Davis threatened him, and often took out a paper from his Pocket and told him to sign that Memorandum, or paper, which would prevent their bringing the deponant to Court, and he the said Davis would be over in a few ~~days~~ weeks in order to have tittles made, if the Deponant found he was Safe in making, the Deponant refused Amany he was inclined, but in order to save the trouble of coming to Court, signed it, which the deponent now believes were tittles as said Davis has made no further application to him on the Subject, which paper the said Davis has never Read to the deponent.

Sworn in open Court. — Perran X Pharrow his mark

Daniel Gaines }
vs }
W[m] Good }

Jury Sworn, to wit.

1. Robert Ellis
2. Richd Cosby
3. Benjamin Fortson
4. John Satterwhite
5. Wm Burch
6. J. Morrison
7. John Darden
8. James Banks
9. Drury Thompson
10. Thomas Napier
11. Richard McGehee
12. John Buckhanan

We the Jury find for the plaintiff twelve pounds, twelve Shillings, and Seven pence, with Cost.

John Buckhanan, Fore^{n}

Ordered, that Thomas Burton, Senr, John Coleman, and Thomas Barton, Junr be and they are hereby appointed Inspectors of the Petersburg Inspection of Tobacco at Oliver's Ware house for the Insuing year, they giving they giving Bond as the Law directs.

Whereupon, the said Thomas Burton, John Coleman, and Thos Burton, Junr, With W^{m}

——

Wm Hatcher, Wm Goode, Thos Burton (Watchie), & John Hubbard, their Securities, Came into Court and Severally acknowledged themselves Indebted to his Excellency, the Governor, and his Successors in Office, in the sum of five Hundred pounds, each to be void on Conditions, that the said Thomas Burton, John Coleman, and Thomas Burton, Junr, do with and truly demean themselves as Inspectors at Petersburgh, Oliver's Warehouse, according to Law, for and During the term of twelve Months.

Thos Burton, John Coleman, Thos Burton, Junr,
Thos Burton (Washatchie), Wm Hatcher, Wm Goode

Wm Allen }
vs }
Andrew Johnson}

I do hereby confess Judgement to the Plaintiff for the Sum of Seven Pounds, fifteen Shillings, and two pence, with Interest, till paid, and Cost.

Test. John Griffin Andrew Johnson

The Court then Adjourned till tomorrow ten o'Clock.

Thursday, 2nd October 1794

Court met, Pursuant to adjournment.

Present, Wm Barnett, James Tait, Evan Ragland, Richardson Hunt, Saml Higginbotham, Esq^{rs}

Archer Burton, the Administrators of the Estate of David Adams, Deceased, Suggested [52]
the propriety of of making Sale of the real Estate od Said Adams, to the Court, which was Ordered to be Entered.

Josiah Lyon }
vs } Case
Wm Daniel }

Nonsuit.

Mathias Mahey & Co. }
vs }
Ric^d Coulter }

Nonsuit.

Fleming Jourdon }
vs }
John Depriest }

I do Confess Judgement to the Plaintiff in this case, for the Just and full Sum of five Pounds, ninteen Shillings, and four Pence, half penny, with Interest, and Cost of Suit, and Stay of Execution Seven Months, 2nd of October 1794.

Saml Blackburn, Def^t Att^y

Wm Stith }
vs }
Thomas Carter }

Jury Sworn (to wit)

1. John Boyd
2. E. Hendrick
3. Thomas Napier
4. William Edwards
5. John Hubbard
6. Thomas Cook
7. William Johnson
8. Charles Smith
9. A. Ponder
10. John Cook
11. Edmond Rowsy

We the Jury find for the plaintiff Seven pounds, ninteen Shillings, and Eight pence.

Thomas Napier

John McEver }
vs }
A. Heard }

Jury Sworn (to wit)

1. Saml King	7. T. Cook
2. Andrew Millican	8. Thos Smith
3. D. Morgan	9. Ri^d Clements
4. Wm Claghorn	10. B. Fortson
5. O. Patterson	11. L. Mosley
6. A. Burton	12. B. Cook

We the Jury find for the plaintiff Seventy pounds Sterling, with Interest.

A. Millican, F.

Major & Sally Allen}
Brock }
vs }
John Thornhill }

The same Jury as in the above Case.

We the Jury find for the plaintiff One Hundred pounds Sterling, with Cost of Suit.

A. Millican, Foreman

Culbird Hudson }
vs }
Administrators of }
James Currier, Dec^d }

The same Jury as in the Case above.

We the Jury find for the plaintiff the Sum of Seventeen Pounds, two Shillings, with Cost.

Thos Napier

John Colley }
vs }
Wm Carter }

The same Jury as in the Case McEver vs A. Head.

We the Jury find for the plaintiff Seventeen Pounds, with Interest and Cost of Suit.

A. Millican, Fore.

Owen Shannon }
vs }
Edw[d] McGarry & }
Rob[t] Meanes }

We Confess Judgement to Owen Shannon, for the Sum of Eight Pounds Specie, with Interest, and Cost, and Stay of Execution till the first of December next. Witness our hands, this 2nd October 1794.

Edw[d] McGarry, W[m] Ward

Benjamin Knox }
vs }
David McCleskey }
& H. Johnson }

The same Jury as in the Case Stith vs Carter.

We the Jury find for the ~~Defendant~~ Plaintiff £5,15,10, with Cost.

Thomas Napier

William Daniel & John Depriest came into Court and acknowledged themselves Security, According to Law. [53]

John Heard }
vs }
W. Blankinship }

The same Jury as in the Case McEver vs Heard.

We the Jury find for the Plaintiff twenty Pounds, Interest and Cost of Suit.

A. Millican, Fore[n]

Edward Wade }
vs } Case
Samuel King }

Nonsuit.

William Dunlap }
vs }
William Thompson }

The plaintiff being three called, not answering, Ordered, that he be nonsuited.

On Motion of Thomas B. Scott, Reuben Lindsay & A. Jarrett, Ordered that the obtain a Licence to keep a tavern at Elbert Court house, they complying with the terms of the Law.

On the petion of James Kidd, Ordered that he obtain Licence to Keep a Publick House at Elbert Court house, he complying with the requisits of the Law. John Depriest and Henry Ross, with James Kidd, came into Court and acknowledged themselves bound in the Sum of fifty pounds unto their honors, the Judges of the Inferior Court. To be void on Conditions, that the Said James Kidd, to do keep an orderly decent house, with good and Sufficient accommodations for travellors, their horses, and attendeans.

On application of John Boyd, Ordered that James McKinsey be bound an apprentice to E. Eavinson, Saddler, untill he Shall arrive to Lawfull Age, to learn the art & mistery of Saddling, on the Said Eli Eavinson's Complying with the Requisits of the Law.

On the application Richard Swisy, Stating to the Court that Nancy and Charles Swisey, Orphans, had not a Comfortable Support.

Ordered, that Richard Swisey be appointed Guardian for Nancy, on his complying with the terms of the Law.

Ordered, that David Brown be appointed Guardian for Charles Swisey, on his Giving Bond as the law Directs.

Francis Gordon }
vs }
Rich[d] Coulter }

Settled.

Geo. Fitzgerald }
vs }
Evan Ragland }

Settled.

James Huling }
vs }
Stephen Heard }

Settled.

The following persons was drawn to Serve on the July at the next term, (to wit)

1. Julian Nail, Sen[r]	8. Thomas Hooker
2. John Morris	9. Abell Howell
3. William Tait	10. John Owin
4. Henry Burton	11. James Brown
5. W[m] Runnolds	12. James Miller
6. John Speirs	13. Ri[d] Steagale
7. John McIntire	14. John

14. John Easter	26. Joseph Ferry	[54]
15. Perron Farrow	27. William Gibbs	
16. Daniel McDonald	28. Sam[l] Morris	
17. W[m] Suttles	29. Sam[l] Bridien	
18. James Hawthon	30. Benjamin Smith	
19. James Varner	31. John Nail	
20. Shervo Harris	32. Jacob Prewitt	
21. Robert Hudleston	33. Jacob Higinbotham	
22. Stephen Guarder	34. Jacob Burton	
23. David McCurdey	35. Henry Collins	
24. Richard Colbert	36. Christopher Herman	
25. Jesse Lathan	37. W[m] Walton	

At an Inferior Court held for Elbert County 31st day of March 1795.

Present, their honors William Barnett, Richardson Hunt, Samuel Higginbotham, Esquires

Court adjourned untill tomorrow ten o'Clock.

Wednesday, 1st April

Court met Pursuant to adjournment.

Present, William Barnett, James Tait, R. Hunt, Samuel Higginbotham

Lee & Lee }
vs }
John Rogers }

Jury sworn, to wit.

1. Wm Tait	7. Wells Thompson
2. Wm H. Tait	8. Wm Head
3. David McCurdy	9. Robt Thompson
4. Peter Wych	10. James Highsmith
5. Thomas Cook	11. John Oliver
6. B. Smith	12. Isaias Harbour

We the Jury find for the defendant.

Robt Thompson, Fore^{n}

James McGinchey }
vs }
P. Pharrow }

Dismissed at Plaintiff Cost.

A. Jourdon }
vs } attachment
James Giles }

Dismissed, Plaintiff Cost.

E. Moore }
vs }
Wm David }

Dismissed, Plaintiff Cost.

John Cunningham }
& H. McDonald }
vs }
Wm Ward }

Dismissed.

Thomas Tait }
vs }
Wm H. Tait }

The Bail below came into Court and acknowledged himself Special Bail.

A. McKleroy }
vs }
E. Brewer & }
L. Black }

The common Bail Came into Court and acknowledged himself Special Bail.

C. Sewell }
vs }
Wm Harbin }

The same as above.

D. Hopkins }
vs }
William Head }

The common Bail below came into Court and acknowledged himself Special Bail.

George Houston }
vs }
John Andrew & }
Thomas B. Scott }

I do hereby confess Judgement to the Plaintiff, George Houston, for the Sum of forty one pounds, Sixteen Shillings Sterling, with Stay of Execution till the first day of Jany next, and Cost of Suit.

Thomas B. Scott

Richardson Hunt } [55]
vs }
Josiah ~~John~~ Adams }

Jury Sworn, to wit.

1. Josep Culbert
2. Thomas Woldridge
7. James Brown
8. Reuben Cook

3. L. McAlpin	9. Wm Head
4. L. Upshaw	10. Thomas Oliver
5. John Blake	11. Wm Cook
6. Josiah Cook	12. F. Gillen

We the Jury find ~~for~~ Three Hundred and Ninty pounds.

Kerkandoll }
vs }
Millican }

Dismissed, at the Defendants Cost.

Thomas Owen }
vs }
John Oliver }

The Same Jury as in The Case, Lee vs Rogers.

We the Jury find for the Pliff. £20,19,1.

Robert Thompson

McCallum & Guardner }
Ass^ee^ Sheriff }
vs }
Isaac Herbert & }
Wm Allen }

I confess a Judgement for the Sum of thirty nine pounds, with Interest from the Third day of March in the year one thousand Seven Hundred and ninety two, with Cost of Suit.

William Allen

McAlpin }
vs } Att^t^
Whitworth }
A. Heard }

The same Jury as in the Case Lee vs Rogers.

We find for the plaintiff ninteen pounds, with Interest from the Thirteenth of October 1790.

Wells Thompson

James Crafford }
vs }
John Patterson }

I do here Confess Judgment for the Sum of Seven pounds, thirteen Shillings, and one penny, and Interest till paid. 1 day of April 1795.

John Mathews

Benjamin Ragland }
vs } Case
James Kidd }

The Jury Case Mentioned.

We the Jury find for the Plaintiff twenty on pounds 6/9½.

Wm Brown, Fore^n^

Ordered, that William Moore be appointed Guardian for William McAlpin, on his complying with the requisits of the Law.

Whereupon, the said Moore with Wm Pullian came into Court and acknowledged themselves Severally bound, unto His Excellency the Governor, in the Sum of two Hundred pounds, for the faithfull performance of the said Moore, as Guardian according to Law.

John Wilson &c. }
vs }
Wm Allen }

I do confess Judgement for the Sum of one Hundred and fifty Seven pounds, three Shillings, & nine pence, half penny, and Cost of Suit, with Stay of Execution four months.

Wm Allen

Ordered, that Josiah Hudson be bound unto James Bell, Esqr untill he arrive to the Age of twenty one years, he giving Security as the Law directs.

On Motion Ordered, that William Barnett, Esquire be appointed Guardian for a negroe woman called Judith, and her Child, Said to be free, In Lieu of Sumner Blackburn, he giving as the Law directs.

Ordered, that Turner Christian be appointed overseer of the Road, from the fork near Larkin Gatewood, to Francis Baties on Deep Creek, and Garrett Turman from thence to James Dudley's Ford on Broad River, and David Roberts from thence to the County line towars Hillhouse's Iron Works. [56]

S. Loveall }
vs } Ejc[t]
J. Spindall }

Dismissed.

Allegany McGuire }
vs }
Murdock Martin }

Settled.

Leroy Pope }
vs }
Benj. Head }

Settled.

W[m] Allen }
vs } Att[t]
Benjamin Head }

Settled.

Elisha Brewer }
vs } Att[t]
A. McKleroy }

The Court then Adjourned till Court in Course.

M. Woods W[m] Barnett, R. Hunt, James Tait

August 4th 1795

Present, Richardson Hunt, Esquire

The following persons were drawn to Serve on Jury at next term, to wit.

1. James Colbert
2. John Palmer
3. James Turman
4. Jesteen Childs
5. Nathan Buttler
6. James Riley
7. John Riley
8. John Morris
9. Robert Woods
10. Geo. Twinmor
11. Dudley Cook
12. John Upshaw
13. John Jones
14. W[m] Akin
15. Isam Jones
16. Tho. Wilkins
17. John Mason
18. Thomas Camron, Jun[r]
19. Elijah Bryant
20. Ben Fortson
21. John Wood
22. John Dabbs
23. Sam[l] Vanhook
24. John Ross
25. Gilbert Marsh
26. Martin Sims
27. Robert Black
28. Isaac David
29. W[m] Gunnels
30. Lolly Dobbs
31. Edw[d] Crews
32. Joseph Moler
33. A. Colron
34. Philip Lewis
35. James Lockhart
36. Benjamin Goss, Sen[r]

Attest. M. Woods

At an Inferior Court held at Elbert Court house the 29th day of September 1795.

Present, William Barnett, R. Hunt, Evan Ragland, James Tait, Samuel Higgenbotham

W[m] Booker }
vs }
John Rinker }

Jury Sworn (to wit)

1. Tho. Akin
2. A. Colson
3. John Upshaw
4. John Jones
5. Dudley Cook
6. James Colbert
7. N. Butler
8. David Martin
9. Joseph Rinker
10. A. Millican
11. John McGowen
12. Jesse White

We the Jury find for the plaintiff 24 Dollars, with Interest, from the time the Note became due, with Cost.

A. Colson

Leroy Pope }
vs }
James Cook } [57]

Jury Sworn, to wit.

1. Philip Lewis	7. Moses Bailey
2. Wm Sharp	8. John Algood
3. Wm Hatcher	9. George Wych
4. James Thurman	10. Wm H. Davis
5. James Coleman	11. L. Black
6. Lewis Phips	12. James Banks

We the Jury find for the plaintiff fifty eight Dollars and Eighty four Cents.

Wm Hatcher

The Court proceed to the appointment of Tobacco Inspectors for the Petersburgh ware house, when Thomas Burton, Senr, John Coleman, and Thomas Burton, Junr was duly Elected.

Mathias Williamson }
vs }
Wm Alexander }

the same Jury as in the case Booker vs Rucker.

We the Jury find for the Defen^d^.

A. Cooper }
vs } Case
Gerrald Walthall }

I do hereby confess Judge^t^ for the Sum of thirty one Dollars and Sixty five Cents, with Stay.

G. Walthall

Thomas Gilmon }
vs }
James Head & }
John McAll }

The same Jury as in the case Pope vs Cook.

We the Jury for the Plaintiff one Hundred and Seventeen Dollars & forty Cents, and Cost. Wm Head and John Pollard acknowledged themselves Sec^y^ for Stay according to Law.

Re^d^ in full Wm Hatcher

William H. Tait }
vs }
Thomas Tait }

I do hereby Confess Judgment for the sum of Seventy Six Dollars and twelve and a half Cents, and Cost, with Stay of Execution untill Christmast next. September 29th 1795

Zimry Tait, for Thos Tait

R. Rutherford }
vs } Debt
Edward McGarry }

Dismissed.

The Court then adjourned untill tomorrow ten o'clock.

Evan Raglan, James Tait, R. Hunt, S. Higginbotham

Wednesday, 30th

Present, as yesterday.

Samuel Blackburn }
vs }
Jonathan Arnold }

By Virtue of Power of Att^y^ to me Directed and incorporated in the within Bond or note, I appear for the defendant and confess Judgment for the Sum of forty one Dollars & Eighty two Cents, with Interest from the date.

Mathews

Robert Bond }
vs } Case
C. Mooney }

Jury Sworn, to wit.

1. N. Buttler	7. Benj. Brown
2. D. Cook	8. John Dailey
3. A. Colson	9. Moses Bailey
4. J. Lockhart	10. J. Alston
5. Wm Sharp	11. Wm Burch
6. Tho. Napier	12. Wm Brawner

We the Jury find for the Plaintiff Sixty four Dollars.

Thos Napier

Saml Blackburn }
vs } Debt [58]
James Head }

By virtue of a Power of Att^{y} hereunto annexed, I do hereby appear for James Head and acknowledge the Service of a Writ and Confess Judgment for the Sum of twenty three Dollars and fifteen Cents, with Interest, from the 20th of May 1795, and Cost of Suit.

John Mathews, Defd^{t} Att^{y}

F. Upshaw }
vs }
John Staples }

Dismissed.

Christopher Sewell }
for John Mathews }
vs } Case
Wm Harbin }

I do hereby Confess Judgement for the Sum of twenty Eight Dollars & Eighty Cents, with Stay of Levy six months, and cost.

W^{m} X Harbin his mark

Test. John C. Walton

Samuel Sewell}
vs } Case
Charles Goss }

Isd.

I do hereby Confess Judgment for the Sum of Sixty three Dollars and Eighty five Cents, with Stay of Execution Six Months.

John C. Walton, Def[t] Att[y]

James Fleming }
vs } Debt
John Patterson }

The Same Jury as in the case Bonds vs Mooney.

We the Jury find for the plaintiff one Hundred and twenty Seven Dollars, Seventy five Cents.

Thomas Napier

David Hopson }
vs }
W[m] Head }

In three different Suits Cont[d] on the Affidavit of the def[t].

Augustus Baldwin }
vs }
Reuben Allen }

In this case, W[m] H. Tait came into Court and acknowledged himself Special Bail, in terms of the Law.

W[m] Puttnam }
vs } Case
Joseph Blackwell }
& R. Banks }

Jury Sworn, to wit.

1. V. Smith	7. Reuben Cook
2. John Staples	8. Benjamin Cook
3. Ric[d] Cosby	9. John Owen
4. R. Easter	10. Tho. Scales
5. B. Fortson	11. Daniel Head
6. Thomas Lam	12. W[m] Aycock

We the Juryors find for the Def[t].

Benj. Cook

Thomas Watkins }
vs } Att[t]
Benj. Head }

Dismissed, at the Def[t] Cost.

John Rhodes for }
A. Jones }
vs }
Joel Crafford }

Georgia, Elbert Inferior

September Term 1795

I do hereby Confess a Judgement on the within ~~Note~~ for the Sum of fifty Seven Dollars, and Stay of Execution till March next.

Joel Crafford

Leroy Pope } [59]
vs } Case
George F. Gerald }

By virtue of the Power to me directed, I appear for the Def[t] and Confess a Judgement for twenty four Dollars and Sixty two Cents.

F. Cosby, Df[t] Att[y]

Violilly Morrison }
vs }
Joseph H. Morrison }

By Virtue of a Power to me directed, I appear for the Def[t] and Confess Judg[t] for three Hundred and twenty Nine pounds, ten Shillings, and four pence Sterling.

F. Cosby, Df[t] Att[y]

A. Vanhook }
vs } Att[t]
W[m] Kilgo }
M. Waters }

The same Jury as in the case Fleming vs Patterson.

We the Jury find for the plaintiff the Sum of Six Hundred and forty one Dollars, with Cost.

Thos Napier

Jesse Thompson }
vs }
Leroy Pope }

Jury Sworn, to wit.

1. B. Cook
2. Thos Lane
3. R. Cook
4. Tho. Scales
5. Wm H. Tait
6. B. Pace
7. Wm Brown
8. Robert Canada
9. L. Mosley
10. Jesse Ross
11. V. Smith
12. John Oliver

We the Jury find for the plaintiff 132 Dollars, twelve and half Cents.

John Oliver

Samuel Blackburn }
vs } Debt
Reuben Allen }

I do appear for the Deft and Confess Judgement for the sum of fifty Dollars, Eighteen Cents, by Virtue of a Power of Attorney given to and Incorporated in the body of the Note declared upon, with Stay of Levy on the usual terms, till the 10th next. 30th September 1795.

Mathews, Att^y

Ordered, that John Hubbard and Thos Cook be appointed Guardians to Mahaley Patsy, Polly Jemima, Crenshaw, who are under age.

On Motion, Ordered that William Arnold be bound unto William Sharp, in terms of the Law, he giving Sec^y, to Learn him the art & Mistery of Farming, and Eighteen Months Schoolling, and when he becomes of mature age, to furnish him with a good Suit of Clothes, and a horse worth twelve Pounds Specie, with a good Saddle and Bridle.

Wm Allen came into Court and acknowledged himself Security according to Law.

At the request of Thomas Oliver and James Certain, they having produced writing undsolved to be a submission of Controversies to Certain

referees, And the award of such referees to become a Rule of Court. [60]

Ordered, that the award of such referees become the Judgment of this Court.

Georgia }
Elbert County }

We, William Barnett, Tho[s] Cook, William Hightower, John Blake, George Cook, taking into consideration the different Controversies Between within named Thomas Oliver and James Certain, are of Opinion that the Said Thomas Oliver do pay unto the within named James Certain One Hundred and forty four Dollars on or before the first day of November next after the date hereof. Given under our hands this 14 September 1795. NB the said Certain making a Lawfull Deed to a certain tract of Land and Mill, when Legally called on by said Oliver, the Said Certain Keeping a Roan Horse now in his Possession, on which he got of Said Oliver.

W[m] Barnett, Thomas Cook, W[m] Hightower,
John Blake, Geo. Cook

Ordered, that John Thompson be appointed Guardian for Thomas Adams, a minor, he giving bond as the Law directs in Such Cases.

The Court then adjourned till tomorrow ten o'Clock.

Thursday, 1st October 1795

The Court met Pursuant to adjournment.

Present, William Barnett, Evan Ragland, Richardson Hunt, Samuel Higginbotham, Esquires

Jesse Thompson }
vs }
Leroy Pope }

Jury, to wit.

1. Elisha Brewer
2. Sam[l] Black
3. John Oliver
4. William Oliver
7. Benj. Cook
8. George Cook
9. G. Henderson
10. J. Colbert

5. B. Pace
6. Thos Cook
11. Jesse Ross
12. Dudley Cook

We the Jury find for the plaintiff the Sum of Ninty Dollars, with Cost of Suit.

Wm Oliver, For^e

George Cook }
vs }
L. Black & }
E. Brewer }

Jury, to wit.

1. John Oliver
2. Wm Oliver
3. B. Pace
4. Wm O. Whitney
5. Allen Daniel
6. W. Blankingship
7. Geo. Henderson
8. James Colbert
9. Jesse Ross
10. D. Cook
11. Wm Head
12. Ben Cook

We the Jury find the Plaintiff the Sum of two Hundred and fourteen Dollars, with Cost of Suit.

Wm Oliver, For^n

The following persons was drawn to Serve on the Jury at the next term, to wit. [61]

1. Jesse Rowell
2. Jesse Green
3. Thos Howell
4. John Wenn
5. John Fleming
6. Jesse Bond
7. Wm Teasly
8. Edwd Lyons
9. Robert Harris
10. Wm Prescott
11. Henry Garner
12. Geo. Averhart
13. John Algood
14. John Algood
15. M. Jones
16. P. Buttler
19. Wm Thompson
20. F. Dobbs
21. A. Hemphill
22. C. Easter
23. A. Thompson
24. James Mason
25. David Adams
26. John Hincle
27. Thomas Jourdon
28. Wm Hall
29. A. Brown
30. J. Hudleston
31. Peter Greenstreet
32. David Franklin
33. George Griffith
34. Saml Spiers

17. Warren Stone
18. John Waterson

35. Drury Allen
36. Wm Haley

Samuel Blackburn }
vs } Debt
W^m^ and R. Allen }

I appear for Wm Allen and Reuben, Esquires and came of the name by Virtue of a power duly proven in Court, do acknowledge the Service of a Writ, in this Case, and do Confess Judgement for the Sum of twenty three Dollars, twenty Nine Cents, with interest till paid, and Clerks Cost, this 30th Sep^t^ 1795, with Stay Levy till 10th Feby 96, on the usual terms.

J. Mathews

Richard Colbert }
vs } Att^t^
Benj. Head }

Settled.

Wm Moss }
vs } Att^t^
Benjn Pollard }

Dismissed.

Wm Allen }
vs } debt
Adam Garr }

Settled.

Shearwood Harris }
vs } Assault
Wm Head }

Settled, Def^t^ Cost.

Commissioners }
vs }
John Rucker }

Settled.

D. Demontroy }
vs } assumsit
E. Brewer }

Dismissed.

Hunt & Stalling }
vs }
Thompson & Watkins }

Dismissed.

Elijah Cook }
vs }
Wm Lane }

dismissed.

Zimry Tait }
vs }
Wm H. Tait }

By consent of Parties, it is Ordered, that all matters of dispute Between the parties, relative to the above Suit, be submitted to the final arbitrament & award of Mathew J. Williams, Robert Thompson, and Thomas Burton, Junr, Esquires, with the Power of umpirage, which Said Award Shall be final and made the Judgment of this Court, provided it be returned to the next Inferior Court. Sep^t 30th 1795

The Court then adjourned till Court in Course.

Wm Barnett, R. Hunt, & E. Ragland, Esquires

At an Inferior Court held at Elberton the 19th day of July 1796. [62]

Present, William Barnett, James Tait, Evan Ragland, R. Hunt, Samuel Higginbotham, Esq^rs

Edward Brewer Came into Court and expressed a desire to be bound unto Robert L. Tait for the purpose of learning the Carpenters trade. Ordered, that he be bound unto the said Tait, on his giving bond as the Law directs.

Thomas Tait made application to the Court for License to keep a Tavern.

Ordered, that the Same be granted, he giving Bond and Sec^y as the Law directs.

On application of David Barnett praying that Thomas Scott, Esquire might be appointed his Guardian. ordered, that the same be granted on his Complying with the terms of the Law.

Polly Stroud came into Court and prayed that John Stroud Might be appointed his Guardian. Whereupon, it id Ordered, that he be appointed.

Wiley Thompson came into Court and made Choice of Middle Woods as his Guardian. Ordered, that he be appointed.

The Court appointed Evan Ragland Guardian for James Thompson, minor, on his giving bond as the Law directs.

William Burch}
vs }
Charles Goss }

Benjamin Goss came into Court and acknowledged himself Special Bail in this Case according to Law.

On the Petition of John Ragland, praying that he might obtain a Licence to keep a Tavern in Petersburgh, ordered that the prayer of the petitioner be Granted on his Complying with the Law.

Admrs of Adams }
vs }
Peter Morris & }
Joseph H. Morris }

Cornelius Sale came into Court and acknowledged himself Special Bail in this Suit, according to Law.

Robert Moon }
vs }
John Millican }

Jury Sworn, to wit.

1. Wm Teasly	7. P. Buttler
2. Henry Gaines	8. Wm Hall
3. A. Hemphill	9. David Frankin
4. A. Brown	10. Wm Haley
5. Jesse Ginn	11. Thomas Oliver
6. E. Lyon	12. Joseph Davis

We the Jury find for the Plaintif thirty nine Dollars, fifty Seven Cents.

Thomas Oliver, Fore[n]

John Parker came into Court and acknowledged himself Security according to Law.

John M. Whitney }
vs }
E. Brewer and }
L. Black }

B. Cook (BR) came into Court and acknowledged himself ~~Security~~ Special Bail in this case, according to Law.

Robert L. Tait, with W[m] H. Tait, came into Court and acknowledged themselves bound unto [63] the Inferior Court of Elbert County, in the penalty of five Hundred Dollars, for his faithfull performance as Guardian for Edmond Brewer, and also to Learn him the art and mistery of house Joiner, to give him Learning Sufficient, also holesome diet, and Cloathing for asad of his Capasity.

W[m] Mitson }
vs }
W[m] Cain }

Robert Moon and Hugh Barr Came into Court and acknowledged himself Special Bail.

The Court proceed to make Choice of Inspectors for the Petersburgh Inspection, When Tho[s] Burton and Thomas Burton, Jun[r] and Charles Taylor was appointed. The Said Thomas Burton and Thomas Burton, Jun[r], with Rob[t] Middleton and James Coleman, acknowledged themselves bound unto his Excellency the Governor, and his Successors in office, in the Sum of fifteen Hundred Dollars, for the faithfull performance of the said Thomas Burton and Thomas Burton, Jun[r] as Inspectors as afore Said, Agreeable to Law.

The Court appointed William Wynn Guardian for Jinsey Eps Thompson, on his complying with the Law.

Ordered, that Nancy Rogers, Relict of John Rogers, be appointed Guardian for her three Children, to wit, Milley, George, and Zilley, when Garrett Turman came into Court and acknowledged himself bound unto the Sum of One Thousand Dollars, for the faithfull performance of the trust as aforesaid.

—

Ordered, that Thomas Woldridge be appointed Overseer of the Road from the fork by Wm Thompson to J. P. Harper.

Ordered, that William Hightower be appointed Overseer of the Road from John P. Harper to the Cross Road, near F. Cook, Esquire.

Jesse Thompson }
vs } Case
James Coleman }

Nonsuit.

Adme^rs^ Adams }
vs } Case
Booker Easter }

Settled.

The Court then adjourned untill tomorrow ten o'Clock.

Wednesday, 20th July 1796

Court met Pursuant to adjournment.

John Buckhanan }
vs }
John Thompson }

~~The same Jury as in the case Moon vs Millican.~~

Jury Sworn, to wit.

1. Jesse Ginn	7. E. Lyon
2. William Haley	8. P. Buttler
3. A. Brown	9. Wm Akin
4. L. Mosley	10. Henry Gaines
5. George Furman	11. Benjamin Browne
6. Wm Teasley	12. J. Cook

We the Jury find for the plaintiff thirty Dollars, thirty Seven and a half Cents, with Interest.

Wm Akin, Foren

William Banks }
vs }
Leroy Pope }

Jury Sworn, to wit.

1. Richard Colbert
2. W. Blankinship
3. M. Turman
4. W. Nunnilee
5. R. Cook
6. Wm Head
7. James Head
8. Trion Harris
9. R. Smith
10. R. Hudleton
11. Thos Cook
12. Thomas Burton
13. E. Cook

We the Jury find for the plaintiff one Hundred and

and Eighty Six Dollars, thirty three Cents, to be Credited by a note of Eighteen pounds Virginia Currency against the said Plaintiff in the hands of the Def^{t} when brought forward. [64]

W. Nunnelee

Harmon Crity }
vs } Case
Leroy Pope }

The same Jury as in the Buckhanan vs Thompson.

We the Jury find for the plaintiff One Hundred and fifty Dollars, with Interest.

Wm Akin, Fore^{n}

George Herston }
vs }
Leroy Pope }

The same Jury as in Crity vs Pope.

We the Jury find for the plaintiff one Hundred and fifty Dollars, with Cost & Interest.

Wm Akin, Fore^{n}

Job Carter }
vs }
Leroy Pope }

The Jury as in the last cause.

We the Jury find for plaintiff one Hundred and Seventy Dollars and twenty five Cents, with Interest.

Wm Akin, Fore^n

Wm Strong }
vs }
Wm Grey }

The same Jury as in the Banks vs Pope.

We the Jury find for the Def^t.

W. Nunnelee

On Motion, Ordered that Thomas Akin be appointed Guardian for Nancy Akin. Robert Middleton with Thomas Akin came into Court and acknowledged themselves bound unto the Judges of said Court, in the Sum of five Hundred Dollars, To be void Conditions that the Said Thomas Akin to well and truly demean himself of the Office above mentioned.

Ordered, that William Aycock be appointed Guardian for Charlotte Easter, when said Aycock and William Hightower Came into Court and acknowledged themselves bound unto the Inferior Court, in the Sum of five Hundred Dollars, to be void on conditions that the said Aycock do well and truly demean himself of the Appointment as aforesaid.

Mathias W^m son }
vs }
Thomas Fortson }

Jury Sworn, to wit.

The same as the Buckhanan vs Thompson. Wm Akin excepted Ri^d Cosby in Lieu thereof.

We the Jury find for the Plff. five Dollars, fifty Cents.

R^ard Cosby

Thomas Hemphill } [65]
vs }
David McCleskey }
& Thomas Rogers }

The Jury as in the Case Strong vs Wm Grey.

We the Jury find for the plaintiff four Hundred and thirty Dollars.

I do Agree to Receive Tittles for the Land }
agreeable to the bond on which this Verdict }
is given if tendered in Six months. }
James McCleskey acknowledged Sec^{y} }
Deed filed 8 Decr 96.

Wm Akin, Fore^{n}

David Hopson }
vs }
Wm Head }

Jury Sworn, to wit.

1. Ric^{d} Colbert
2. W. Blankenship
3. M. Tureman
4. Thomas Burton
5. Wm Nunnelee
6. R. Cook
7. B. Brown
8. N. Tuttle
9. Robert Smith
10. Robert Hudleston
11. Thos Cook
12. E. Cook

We the Jury find for the defendant.

Wm Nunnelee

D. Hopson }
vs }
Wm Head }

The Same Jury and Verdict.

Augustus Baldwin }
vs } Case
Reuben Allen }

I confess Judgment for the Sum of fifty five Dollars, fifty Seven Cents, Elbert Inferior Court.

R. Allen

Thomas Scott came into Court and acknowledged himself Sec^{y} for Stay of Levey.

John F. Flournoy }
vs }
John M. Whitney }

Jury Sworn, to wit.

1. James Tuttle	7. Wm Fortson
2. John Wingfeld	8. James Carter
3. Benjamin Smith	9. Wm Gibbs
4. John Montgomery	10. Thos Carter
5. Benjn Cook	11. John Smith
6. James Alston	12. A. McGuire

We the Jury find for the plaintiff forty three Dollars, seventy five Cents.

B. Cook

Richd Colbert for }
Ch^s Hudson }
vs }
Wm Head }

The Same Jury as in the case Banks vs Leroy Pope. Ric^d Colbert excepted Tho. Penn in Lieu.

We the Jury find for the plaintiff Sixty five Dollars, and Seventy five Cents.

Wm Head acknowledged himself Sec^y.

W. Nunnelee

Henry Tillury }
vs } Case
Henry Jackson }

The Same Jury as before.

We the Jury find for the plaintiff forty Dollars.

W. Nunnelee

John Pollard }
vs } Case
Wm Davis }

We the parties Litigant in the above Case, do Multiply agree to refer the Same to Stephen Heard, James Alston, James Banks, and William Moore, Senr, whose award Shall be entered up as the Judgement of said Court, and in case they Should not agree, we do authorize the aforesaid referees to allow a fifth person as umpire, whose Sole award Shall be the Judgement of Court as aforesaid, the award to be returned into Court on or before the first day of the next term Given

Given under our hands 20th July 1796. [66]

M. W^m son, Att^y Plf.
Wm Davis

On Motion, Ordered, that William Thompson (R) be appointed Guardian for Elizabeth and Tabitha Thompson, he complying with the requisits of the Law.

Ordered, that Lewis Mosley be appointed Guardian for Patsy Thompson.

Ordered, that Booker Easter be appointed Guardian for Thompson Adams.

James Banks }
vs } Case
Thomas Barren }

I do authorize M. W^m son, Esqr to Confess Judgement for the principal and Interest of the within note, with Stay of Execution untill the first day of January 1797.

Thomas B Barren his mark

Colin Reed }
vs } Case
M. Wilcox }

Settled.

Wm J. Hobby }
vs } Case
Wm Lane }

Settled.

Hannah Martin }
vs } Case
Leroy Pope }

Settled.

—

David Hillhouse }
vs } Case
Andrew Hemphill }

Dismissed.

John P. Wagnon }
vs } Case
Wm Bibb }

Abated by the death of the Defendant.

John Wilson & Co }
vs } Cov^t^
Thos & James Oliver }

The plaintiff being three times called, and not answering, ordered that he be nonsuited.

John Wilson & Co }
vs } Cov^t^
Thomas Oliver }

The same order as in the above case.

Joseph Akin }
vs }
Wm Goode }

Abated, by the death of the Plaintiff.

The Court then adjourned untill tomorrow ten o'Clock.

Thursday, 21st July 1796

Court met Pursuant to adjournment.

Present, William Barnett, Richardson Hunt, Evan Ragland, Saml Higginbotham

Middleton Woods } [67]
vs }
John M. Whitney }

The common Bail below George Cook came into Court and acknowledged himself Special bail for the Def[t] in this case, and that he would render his body in discharge or pay the Condemnation.

E. Hightower }
vs }
Rob[t] Hudleston }
et al }

E. Hightower }
vs }
Rob[t] Hudleston }
et al }

W[m] Head came into Court and acknowledged himself Special Bail for the Defen[t] in the above cases and that he would pay the condemnation money for them or Render their Bodies in discharge.

Benjamin Cook }
vs }
John M. Whitney }

Evan Ragland, the Common Bail, acknowledged himself Special Bail, for the defendant in this case, and that he would pay the Condemnation money for him, or render his body in discharge.

John Lowrey }
vs } Slander
W[m] Spiers }

Nonsuit.

Steward for }
Houston }
vs }
G. Walthall }

Bail Bond assigned.

—

Hillory Hendrick }
vs }
James Kidd }

John Rucker, the Bail below, came into Court and acknowledged himself Special Bail for the Defendant in this Case, and that would the Condemnation money for him, or render his body in discharge.

Reuben Lindsay }
vs }
John Doss }

Settled.

On the petition of James McDonald, praying some relief migh be Grant on Act. of his old age and infirmness, whereupon it is the Opinion of the Court that the Said McDonald be provided for out of the public funds, if any.

Joseph Neal and Richd Tyner, appointed by the Court Commissioners to view the ground whereon a road is proposed to run (to wit) from The Scales on Savannah River to Elbert Court House, and to report the Conveniency, or inconveniency, of such Road, Reported as follows, that a Road be opened from Said Scales to Arnold Mills, to Richd Tyner, to Col^o Higginbotham, and thence to the Court House, and that Josiah Dabbs be Overseer over the Road from Scales to Bigg Cedar Creek, John Ross from thence to T. Tyners, and Ri^d Bonds from thence to S. Higginbotham, and Thomas Carter from thence to the ~~Beginning~~ Court House.

Ordered, that the Report be agreed to by the Comm^rs.

On petition of Claibourn Webb, praying that a Road might be opened from his ferry to Franklin Courthouse. [68]

Ordered, that Crisley Deadwelder and John Crowder be appointed Commissioners to View and report to the next Court the propriety of opening Such Road.

Ordered, that David Martin be appointed Overseer over the Road leading from the Court House to Fish Dam Ford B. River, in lieu of John Blake.

Ordered, that Archelies Jarrett be appointed Overseer of the Road from the Court house to Falling Creek, towards Webbs Ferry, And Hezekiah Gray from thence to Webbs Ferry.

The Judges of the Inferior Court of Elbert County, Gentlemen, finding the Goal of the County much out of order, So that I cannot take the Responsibility of prisoners on the Office of Sheriff, I am under the Necessity of Entering this my Protest against the Same.

With due respect, I am yours, &c.

Robert Cosby

Ordered, that George Cook be appointed Constable in Cap[t] Hatcher's District, Nathan Bonds in Cap[t] Blackwell, William Brawner in Staples, R. Cook Burton, Thomas Penn Higginbotham, L. Pace in Shields, Jacob Odem in Crows, James Walker Allens, who came forward and was duly qualified.

Ordered, that James Bell, Esq[r] be allowed Eight Dollars, out of the Money arising from the Sales of Lotts, for his trouble for nursing M[rs] Spurlock, while Sick and for burial expenses.

The Court then adjourned till Court in Course.

William Barnett, R. Hunt, Evan Ragland, Sam[l] Higginbotham

At an Inferior Court begun and Continued at Elbert Court House, the 19th day of December 1796.

Present, their honors William Barnett, Evan Ragland, R. Hunt, S. Higginbotham, Esquires

H. Stuart for }
Josiah Houston }
vs } Case
Gerald Walthall }

Gerald Walthall & Thomas B. Creagh came into Court and acknowledged themselves Special Bail, in the Above case in terms of Law.

M. Woods

Gerald Walthall
Thomas B. Creagh

John Glass } [69]
vs } Case
John M. Whitney }

I do hereby confess Judgment, to the plaintiff, for the Sum of Seventy Dollars, ninty one ¼ Cents, with Cost, Stay of Execution three months.

Tho[s] P. Carnes

John M. Whitney
19th Dec[r] 1796

William McCune }
vs } Attachment
James Cook }

Dismissed.

On the petition Robert Martin and Others.

Ordered, that there be a publick ferry established on Leroy Pope's Land, Opposit to Robert Martin's Ferry, landing in behalf of said Martin, and that there be a Road opened, from Said Landing into the Road Leading from Petersburgh, up Savannah & Broad Rivers.

Ordered, also that John Coleman be overseer to open and keep the Same in Repair.

Ordered, that James Ware, John McKee, Garrett Turman, & Absalom Stinchcomb be appointed Commissioners, to lay out a Road from Scull Shoal on Broad River, to Elbert Court House, Also a Road from Newtons Meeting house, to Elbert Court house, Crossing at Tuttle Shoal, and Report the propriety or impropriety of the Same, to the next Inferior Court.

—

Ordered, that Joseph Neil be appointed overseer of the Road from Lightwood Log Creek, on the Augusta Road, from thence to the fork near John Cunningham's, and George Rogers from thence to McGary's ford on Cold Water, William Alexander from thence to Vanns Creek, Richard Colbert from thence to the Beaver dam Creek, near James Alston's.

Ordered, that Jacob Prewitt, John Jones, Webb Kidd, & Thomas Fortson be appointed Commissioners to lay out a Road, from Middleton's Ferry, to Elbert Court House, and report to the next Court, the propriety or impropriety of the Same.

Archibald Burton, Administrator of the Estate of David Adams, Deceased, appeared in Court & shewed Satisfactory Cause to the Court, why the Real Estate Should be Sold, and he having complied with the in this regard, by advertising in the publick papers the application made for the Sale thereof. It is therefore, Ordered, that the said Archibald Burton, administrator as aforesaid, be and he is hereby authorized to dispose of the Real estate of the said Deceased, in the Manner pointed out by Law, and return an amount of the Sales so made to the proper office.

The Court then adjourned untill tomorrow ten o'Clock.

Tuesday, 20th December [70]

Present, the honorable William Barnett, James Tait, Richardson Hunt, Evan Ragland, Esquires

John Skelton Came into Court & was qualified as Constable for Capt Scales District.

James Shockly }
vs }
Stephen Hanes, Ralph }
Owens, Thomas Woodward, }
Benj[n] Howard, John Files, }
& Harry Files }

We, Ralph Owens, Tho[s] Woodward & Benjamin Howard and Elijah Owens, Nehemiah Howard, and Thomas Scales, Securities, Acknowledged ourselves Bound to the Plaintiff, in the Sum Mentioned in the Sheriffs Bond, on this condition, if the defendants Shall be Cast in this Suit, they the defendants will pay the Condemnation money, or Surrender themselves as the Law Directs, or will do it for them, taken and acknowledged in Court. A. D. December 20th 1796.

Ralp Owens, Benjamin Howard, Thomas Woodward,
Elijah Owens, Thomas Scales, Nehemiah Howard

NB Stephen Haynes, principal, and Moses Haynes, Security, acknowledged themselves as above.

Stephen Haynes, Moses Haynes

Mary Patterson }
vs }
John Patterson }

Dismissed.

Mary Patterson }
vs }
John Patterson }

Dismissed.

A. Burton & }
James Adams }
vs }
Peter Morrison & }
J. H. Morrison }

Cornelius Sale, Special Bail in the above Case, came into Court and delivered Peter Morrison up to the Sheriff.

Zimry Tait }
vs }
Wm H. Tait }

Jury Sworn, to wit.

1. Robert Canada
2. Francis Coulter
3. James Arnold
4. Middleton Fannin
5. Edmond Lowry
6. John Cook
7. John M. Whitney
8. William Brewer
9. George Turman
10. Archer Burton
11. Robert Hudleston
12. Isaac Coker

The Jury find for the defendant.

John M. Whitney

M. Woods }
vs }
John M. Whitney & }
Geo. Cook, S. Bail }

Judgment Confessed for the Sum of one Hundred & thirty five Dollars, with legal Interest thereon, from the first day of October Seventeen Hundred Ninty five, untill paid, with Cost of Suit.

Signed, John Griffin, for Defendant.

John M. Whitney } [71]
vs }
Jeremiah Cleveland }

Judgement by default opined and the Defendant to Stand on a Common appeal. amen.

Thomas Woodlief }
vs }
Walker Richardson }

Jury Sworn, to wit.

1. Richmond Cosby
2. Josiah Cook
3. James Alston
7. M. J. Williams
8. William Hall
9. John Cook

4. John Hubberd
5. Dudlee Cook
6. Tho[s] Akin
10. Martin Turman
11. Thomas Doogles
12. Zimry Tait

We the Jury find for the plaintiff Eight Hundred and twenty nine Dollars & Sixteen Cents, and Cost, & Stay Six months.

John Hubberd, Foreman

by consent, benefit of appeal waved.

William Burch}
vs }
Charles Goss }

Jury Sworn, to wit.

1. Robert Canady
2. F. Coulter
3. James Arnold
4. Thomas Cook
5. Edw[d] Lowry
6. John Cook
7. John M. Whitney
8. William Brewer
9. George Turman
10. Archer Burton
11. Robert Hudleston
12. Isaac Colter
13. William Oliver

We the Jury find for the plaintiff the Sum of ninty Dollars, Interest and Cost.

W[m] Oliver, Foreman

The party prayed an appeal, when Robert Hudleston acknowledged Sec[y] in terms of the Law.

John Hubberd }
vs }
James Kidd }

The same Jury as in the Case Woodlief vs Walker Richardson.

Some of the Jury failing to answer, the Same was declared to be a mistrial.

A. McKleroy }
vs }
George Cook }

I, William Oliver, Security, do acknowledge myself Indebted to the Plaintiff in the Sum mentioned in the Sheriffs Bond, on this Condition, that if the defendant shall be cast in this Suit, that the defendant will Pay the Condemnation Money or Surrender himself as the Law Directs, or I will do it for him, Taken and acknowledged in Court.

Test. M. Woods Geo. Cook, Wm Oliver

Edward Walthall made application to the Court for a Licence to keep a tavern on the Road, about three miles from Petersburgh.

Ordered, that the Same be Granted, on his Complying with the Law, When Joel Butler came into Court and acknowledged himself bound in the Sum of Two Hundred & fifty Dollars, to be void on Conditions, that the Said Walthall do keep a Good orderly house according to Law.

M. Woods Edwd Walthall, Joel Butler

Epaphroditus Hightower }
vs }
Robert & Joseph Hudleston }
& William Blake } [72]

The Same }
vs }
The Same }

The Same Jury as in the Case Burch vs Goss, Reuben Cook & Edwd Goode excepted, in lieu of Robert Hudleston and Thomas Cook.

One of the Jury failing to answer, the Same was declared to be a mistrial.

On Petition, Ordered, that Garrett Walthall, Junr be appointed Guardian for Isham Thompson, Minor, he Complying with the Law in Such Cases, When Thomas B. Creagh came into Court and acknowledged himself Security in the Sum of One thousand Dollars, for the faith performance as above according to Law.

Gerrard Walthall, Tho. B. Creagh

William Milton }
vs }
William Cain }

Robert Moon, Special Bail for in this Case, delivered up his Principal. Whereupon, Richard Cain became Special Bail, in the Room and Stead of the Said Robert Moon.

Test. M. Woods   Ric[d] Kain

Ordered, that George Cook be appointed Guardian for Ginsey Eps Thompson, in Lieu of William Wynn, he Complying with the Law in Such Cases, When Thomas Cook came into Court and acknowledged himself bound in the Sum of One Thousand Dollars for his faithfull performance as above.

M. Woods   George Cook, Thomas Cook

Eliza Williams, Adm[x] }
vs }
William Elliott }

I do confess Judgment to the plaintiff for the Sum of one Hundred and ninty three Dollars and two Cents, with Cost of Suit, and three months Stay ~~of Execution~~, and this Judgment may be discharged during the Said three months by Barr Iron at Six pence per pound, Cows and Calves at three pounds, provided they are prime, and likely horses, to be Valued by two men to be Chosen indifferently by John Griffin And the defendant, the Said Articles to be delivered in Washington, and as near as may be in an equal proportion, that is to Say, the whole may be discharged in Bar Iron, but if in Cattle & Horses, Rendered then an equal part must be in Barr Iron and equal one in Cows and Calves, and in horses.

Tho[s] P. Carnes

Ferdinand Finizer }   [73]
vs }
Joseph Wilson }

I do hereby Confess Judgment to the plaintiff for the Sum of Eleven Hundred ninty three Dollars, twenty three Cents, & Cost, and Interest from the first day of January 1796.

Test. John Griffin   Joseph Wilson

Ordered, that there be a Road from Shaklefords Ferry, to the Cherokee ford on Savannah River, and that James Oliver, William Davis, and Joseph Deadwiler be and they are hereby Appointed Commissioners of the Same.

Administrator Adams }
vs }
Peter Morrison & }
J. H. Morrison }

I do hereby confess Judgment to the plaintiff for the sum of forty four Dollars and Sixty two Cents, and Cost of Suit, with four months Stay of Execution.

Test. John Griffin

Peter Morrison, for Self
& J. H. Morrison

John Hubberd }
vs } Case
Chesley Morris & }
Wm Wynn }

Judgment Confessed for forty one Dollars fifty Cents.

Wm Winn

Test. John Mathews

The Court then adjourned untill ten O'clock.

Wednesday 21st

The Court met pursuant to adjournment.

Present, their honors William Barnett, James Tait, Evan Ragland, R. Hunt, & S. Higginbotham, Esqr^s^

James Shockley }
vs } Case
Benjamin Howard }

I, Benjamin Howard, and we, Nehemiah Howard and Thomas Scales, the Securities, Acknowledged ourselves bound to the Plaintiff in the Sum ~~of~~ mentioned in the Sheriffs Bond, on this Condition, that if the defendant Shall be cast in the Suit, he the defendant will pay the Condemnation or Surrender himself up as the Law Directs, or we will do it for him, taken and acknowledged in Court. A. D. Decr 21 1796.

Benj. Howard, N. Howard, Thos Scales

Joseph Pulliam }
vs }
Henry Collins }

Dism^d^.

James Cooper }
vs }
John M. Whitney }

I do hereby confess Judgment to the Plaintiff for the Sum of thirty four Dollars and twenty Eight Cents.

John M. Whitney

John M. Whitney } [74]
vs }
L. Black & E. Brewer }

Dismised.

Hugh Stewart }
vs }
Gerrard Walthall }

I confess Judgment for the Sum of thirty Seven Dollars, and Costs, and Stay Nine Months.

Gerrard Walthall

William Milton }
vs }
Wm Cain }

Dismised.

Adm^rs Adams }
vs }
David Thurman }
et al }

Jury Sworn to wit.

1. Richmond Cosby
2. Josiah Cook
3. Dudley Cook
4. Thomas Akin
5. M. J. Williams
6. John Cook
7. Martin Turman
8. Joseph Rucker
9. L. Mosley
10. Thomas Scales
11. Thomas Smith
12. George Cook

We the Jury find for the plaintiff four Hundred and Eighty Dollars fourteen Cents.

M. Williams

Benjamin Cook }
vs }
John M. Whitney }

I do hereby confess Judgment to the plaintiff for the Sum of one Hundred and twenty one Dollars and thirty one Cents, and Cost of Suits, and Stay four months.

Test. John Griffin John M. Whitney

Ordered, that Zimry Tait, Thomas Doogles, Edward Goode, George Turman, & Robert Canada be fined fifty Cents for their nonattendance as Jurors.

Ordered, that Wiley Thompson be bound unto Middleton Woods untill he arrive to the Age of twenty One, he Complying with the Law, in Such Cases made and provided.

William Lane }
vs }
Joseph Blackwell }

Jury Sworn, to wit.

1. James Oliver	8. E. Cook
2. Thomas Cook	8. Isham Morgan
3. Walker Napier	9. Joseph Downer
4. J. Rucker	10. Thomas Burton
5. Dozier Cook	11. Edmond Lowry
6. James Arnold	12. Benjamin Brown

We the Jury find for the plaintiff ninty Eight Dollars.

Walker Napier

Epaphroditus Hightower }
vs } Case
Robert Hudleston }
et al }

The Same }
vs } Case
The Same }

We do agree to Submit all Matters in dispute to the award and determina

tion of William Barnett, Richardson Hunt, & Evan Ragland, Esquires, and there award, or [75] any two ~~of them~~ to be made the Judgment of the Court, and entered at this term, Stay of Execution is to be given for two ~~Months~~ thirds of the Judgment for two months, and for the balance untill the last of November next.

Test. John ~~Griffin~~ Mathews Epap[h] Hightower, Robert Hudlston

We, William Barnett, R. Hunt, and Evan Ragland, do award to Epaphroditus Hightower Three Hundred and Seventy four Dollars, with Cost of Suit, from the Said Joseph Hudleston. Given under our hands and Seals. this 22nd December 1796.

W[m] Barnett, R. Hunt, E. Ragland

On petition of an number of the Inhabitants of the upper end of this County.

Ordered, that James Camron, Henry Gragg, and James Hawthon be appointed Commissioners to view and layout a Road from Said Graggs, the most direct Way Towards Franklin Court house, to the County line, and report the Same to the next Court.

Sarah Tarondell }
et al }
vs }
Thomas Carter }

Dismised.

Benjamin Cook }
vs }
John Thompson }

Dismised.

Hillery Hendricks }
vs }
James Kidd }

In this Case, it appeared that a note of hand, on which this ~~Suit~~ action is founded is lost, and the Subscribing Witness appeared to be in a dangerous State of Health, it being doubtful whether he will Survive untill the next term, the Counsel for the defendant consented, It is ordered by the

Court, that the examination of James Bell, the Subscribing Witness aforesaid, be examined as to the Identity and ~~Condents~~ Contents of the Said Bond.

Court adjourned untill tomorrow ten ofClock.

Wm Barnett, R. Hunt, Evan Ragland, James Tait,
Sam Higginbotham

Sherod Morris }
vs }
Sally Morris & }
Isaac Morris }

We do hereby confess a Judgement for Sherod Morris for the Sum of Three Hundred Seventy five Dollars & thirty Seven ½ Cents, with Interest and Cost, the 21 day of Decr 1796.

Sally X Morris her mark
Isaac X Morris his mark

At an Inferior Court held at Elbert Court house the 19th day of July 1797. [76]

Present, William Barnett, James Tait, R. Hunt, E. Ragland, S. Higinbotham, Esquires

J. Hutchings }
vs }
James Tait }

Settled.

John R. Ragland }
vs } attachment
Benjamin Gant }

Jury Sworn to wit.

1. Samuel Spiers	7. Josiah Sarten
2. Thomas Akin	8. James Buttler
3. A. Thompson	9. Thomas Napier
4. James Brown	10. R. L. Tait
5. John Brown	11. Saml Reynolds
6. James Huff	12. John Lowry

We the Jury find for the plaintiff ninty three dollars, thirty Six Cents.

Tho[s] Napier, Fore[n]

Avington McKleroy }
vs }
George Cook }

Nonsuit.

John Bell }
vs }
Francis Coulter }

Jury Sworn, to wit.

1. James Sutton	5. W[m] Hatcher
2. Josiah Cook	6. Isham Morgan
3. Benjamin Brown	7. George Turman
4. Robert Middleton	8. Burket Green

---

9. George Cook	11. Walker Richardson
10. Gilbert Barden	12. Andrew Cunningham

We the Jury find for the plaintiff Sixty five Dollars.

W[m] Hatcher, Fore[n]

William Black }
vs }
William Daniel }

The Same Jury as in the above case.

We the Jury find for the plaintiff ninty one dollars twenty five cents.

Geo. Cook

Felix Gilbert }
vs }
John Carrell }

I do hereby confess Judgement on the within note for Sixty one dollars and twenty five Cents. Witness my hand the ninth day of July 1797.

Test. P. Early John X Carrell his mark

The Court proceeded to the appointment of a Constable in Cap[t] Odem district, when Robert Moon was appointed, In Captain Cowdons district Thomas Griffin, in Cap[t] White District George Cook, in Cap[t] Burtons district Reuben Cook, in Cap[t] McAlpin district John Murrah, in Cap[t] Shields James Alexander, in Cap[t] Alexander's District Frederick McGuire.

The Court proceeded to the Choice of Inspectors at Olivers Ware house, When Thomas Burton, Sen[r], Thomas Burton, Jun[r], and Charles Taylor was appointed.

And, for Watkin's Warehouse, when John Coleman, William Reynolds, and William [77]
Hatcher was appointed.

Middleton Woods }
vs }
William Carter }

I, William Carter, the defendant, and John Wilhite, Security, do acknowledge ourselves bound unto the plaintiff the sum mentioned in the Sheriff's bond, that if he, William Carter, the defendant, Should be cast in the above Suit, that he ~~would~~ will pay the condemnation money, or surrender himself as the law directs, or I will do it for him, taken in Court.

W[m] Carter, John Wilhite

Ordered, that W. A. D. Ewing be appointed Guardian for Charles Ewing, minor, he complying with the law in Such cases.

James Ewing made choice W. A. D. Ewing as his guardian, Ordered, that he be and is hereby appointed.

Ordered, that Moses Haynes be appointed guardian for Six minors, children of Stephen Haynes, Dec[d], on his Giving bond as the law directs.

On the petition of Robert L. Tait praying that he might obtain a licence to retail Spirituous liquors at his own house. Ordered, that the Same be granted, he complying with the requisits of the Law.

On the petition of Hugh McDonald, Ordered, that he obtain a licence to keep Tavern at his own house, he complying with the Law in such Cases.

John Pollard }
Att^{y} for Major Pollard }
vs }
William Davis }

We, the referees appointed by order of Court, do find award for the plaintiff twenty three dollars and fifty cents.

Wm Moon
James Banks
James Alston, Senr

James Shockley }
vs }
Elijah Owens & }
N. Howard }

The Same }
vs }
Stephen Haynes }
et al }

By consent of parties, all matters of dispute relative to the Above Suits, are refered to the award to the arbitrament and final decision of Hugh McDonald, Thomas Gilbert, John Conner, Nimon Barrett, James Tait, John Tipkens, and Daniel Varner, their award ~~to be final~~, or a majority of them, making the Same to be final and conclusive, between the parties, their award to be made in writing, under their hands and Seals, to the Clerk of this Court, on or before of the first day of the next term, and become a Judgement of the Said Court, and it is further agreed that if either of the said arbitrators Should depart This life, or refuse to act, then others are to be nominated, to be approved by both the consenting parties, and the said arbitrators Shall not proceed in the

the aforesaid investigation untill both parties agree that they prepared, the Said arbitrators [78]
to meet and adjourn from time to time, untill their Ward Shall be made up, and they are to give the parties notice of the time and place of their meeting.

M. Williamson, Plf^{s} Att^{y}
Walton & Early, Def^{t} Att^{y}
July 19th 1797

Chrisley Deadwilder and John Crowder, who was appointed Commissioners, to View the way in which a road was proposed to be opened, from Webbs ferry towards Franklin Court House. Reported favorable.

Ordered, that there be road Opened, and that Jones Broach be appointed Overseer, from the ferry to doves Creek, and William Brawner from thence to Absalom Stinchcomb's, and Jesse Statham from thence to John Smith's, and Moses Davis from thence to the County line.

Ordered, that John Montgomery be appointed Overseer of the road, in room of James McDonald.

Ordered, that Thomas Tait be appointed overseer in lieu of William Haley.

Ordered, that A road be opened from front Street, Petersburg, through the Lott N° 37, in a direct line to Savannah River, and that William Goode and John R. Ragland be and they are hereby appointed Overseers to lay out and keep the Same ~~and keep~~ in repair.

——

On the petition of William Carmical, Stating that in an unfortunate reencounter he had apart of his Ear bit of, which greatly disfigures him, and being fearfull that provided he travels or removes out of the neighbourhood, where he at present resides, it may create doubts whether the said misfortune might not be considered as a punishment for Some felony Commited by him, and Prays the honorable the Inferior Court to permit the Promissor to be entered upon the Records of their Court, it appearing to the Satisfaction of the Court, that the right ear of said Wm Carmical was bit of as Stated by him.

It is ordered that the premises be admitted to record.

The Court then adjourned till tomorrow ten o'Clock.

Thursday, 20th

The Court met pursuant to adjournment.

Present, as Yesterday.

John M. Whitney }
vs } attachment
Jeremiah Cleveland }

Dismised.

Hillery Hendricks }
vs }
James Kidd }

Dismised, at the defendant Cost.

Ordered, that Lee Pace, an infirm person, be exempted from paying a Poll Tax.

Ordered, that William Barnett, Esquire be appointed guardian for Lucy Moore, on his [79]
complying with the Law in Such cases.

Harris & Carter }
vs } Case
Robert Buckner }

John Henley }
vs } Case
John Buckner }

I, the defendant, and we, the Securities, do acknowledge ourselves indebted to the plaintiff in the Sum Mentioned in the Sheriff's bond, on both of the above cases, that if the defendant Should be cast, that he, the defendant, would pay the Condemnation money, or Surrender himself as the Law directs, or we will do it for him. Taken and acknowledged in Court.

Robert Brukner, James Wright, Jacob Dyer

Mathias Williamson }
vs }
Joseph Rucker }

Jury Sworn, to wit.

1. Samuel Spiers
2. James Brown
3. A. Cunningham
4. W. Richardson
5. Geo. Alexander
6. Robt L. Tait
7. James Huff
8. Thomas Akin
9. Saml Runnolds
10. James [illegible]
11. John Brown
12. A. Thompson

We the Jury find for the plaintiff Eleven Dollars twenty Cents.

Robert L. Tait

Reuben Lindsay acknowledged himself Sec^y for Stay of levy according to Law.

John Hubberd }
vs }
James Kidd }

Jury Sworn, to wit.

1. Benjamin Brown
2. David Martin
3. John Lowry
4. James Sutton

---

5. Benjamin Goss
6. John Patterson
9. Jere Cook
10. Samuel Clarke

7. Thomas Cook
8. Isham Morgan
11. John Spiers
12. Josiah Sartin

We the Jury find for the plaintiff $109.39.

John Spiers

Gerrard Walthall }
vs }
George Dardin }

Settled.

Thomas Napier }
vs }
Geo. Anderson }

Jury sworn, to wit.

1. Sam[l] Spiers
2. James Brown
3. Aber[illegible]
4. W. Richardson
5. Geo. Alexander
6. Robert L. Tait
7. [illegible] Buttler
8. John Brown
9. Alexander Thompson
10. James Huff
11. Thomas Akin
12. Samuel Runnolds

We the Jury find for the Plaintiff fifteen dollars.

R. L. Tait

James Allen }
vs }
M. Woods }

Jury Sworn, to wit.

1. Drury Bradley
2. James Sutton
3. Isham Morgan
4. Francis Higginbotham
5. Josiah Sartin
6. Sam[l] Clark
7. Josiah Cook
8. John Spiers
9. David Martin
10. John Lowry
11. Benjamin Goss
12. George Cook

We the Jury are of Opinion that the horse died with a disease which was prevailing on him before the defendant received him, therefor find for the defendant.

George Cook

Ezra Morris and Washington Morris and Clara Morris came into Court and made choice of John Higginbotham as their Guardian.

Ordered, that he be appointed, he complying with the law.

The Court made choice of John Higginbotham as guardian of dandridge Morrison and [80]
Francis Morrison, he giving bond as the law directs in Such cases.

Charles Williamson }
vs }
John M. Whitney }

I, the defendant, and I, the Security, Acknowledge ourselves bound unto the plaintiff in the Sum mentioned in the Sheriff's bond, that if I, the defendant, Should be cast, that he the defendant will pay the condemnation money, or surrender himself as the law directs, or we will do it for him, taken and acknowledged in open Court.

John M. Whitney
James Wright

William Chisolm }
vs |
John M. Whitney }

I, the defendant, and the Security acknowledge ourselves bound unto the plaintiff in the Sum mentioned in the Sheriff bond, that if he the defendant Should be Cast, that he the defendant will pay the Condemnation, or Surrender himself as the law directs, or we will do it for him.

John M. Whitney
James Wright
John Cunningham

Ordered, that William Jarvis be bound unto Robert Martin untill he arrives to the Age of twenty one to learn the art & mistery of house Joiner, he the Said Martin giving bond and Security for his compliance as above.

Ordered, that the Clerk do refund the money arising from the Sale of Estrays, Hoggs taken up by James Banks, which was proven to be the property

—

of James M. J. Williams, After deducting the expense on the Same.

On the petition of Thomas Oliver, praying that he may Obtain a Licence to keep tavern at his own house on Beaverdam Creek.

Ordered, that the prayer be granted, on his Complying with the terms of the Law.

Jacob Dyer presented a petition praying license to retail Spirituous liquors in Elberton at his own house. Whereupon, it is ordered that he Obtain a licence in complying with the law in Such cases.

Ordered, that the following persons be appointed Constables for the present year, to wit. James Sutton, John Spiers for Capt Barnetts District, Stephen Haynes for Capt Shires District, Robert Moon for Capt Odems Dist., Edward Clarke for Capt Hudsons district, John Brown for Capt Whites District.

Ordered, that Thomas Rogers be appointed Guardian for Mary, Elizabeth, Obedience, and John Rogers, minors, he complying with the Law in Such Cases.

Upon the petition of John Wilhite and Mildred Wilhite, it is ordered that they be appointed guardians of Thomas Grimes and Patsy Grimes, Minors, they first giving Sec^{y} in the Sum of four thousand dollars, in terms of the Act, in Such cases made and provided.

Upon the petition of William Grimes, a minor, upwards of the age of fourteen years.

It is Ordered, that Thomas B. Scott be appointed

his Guardian, the said Scott first giving bond, with Security in the Sum of twenty five [81]
hundred dollars, in terms of the law, in Such cases made and provided.

Ordered, that there be a road Opened, from the furnace road, near the head of Skull, to Elbert Court house, Crossing Broad River at Denneys ferry, and that George Manifee be appointed Overseer of the Same in Capt McKee's District, James Vineyard in Capt Cowdens, Thomas Mays in Capt Shields, Turner Christian and William Creddington in Capt Higginbotham District.

On a petition of a number of Inhabitants of Elbert County, Ordered, that there be a road Opened and kept in repair, taken out at James McGowins old ferry road, down to Alexanders at the mouth of Cold Water Creek, and from thence into Augusta road, the nearest and best way, And, that William Alexander and John McGowin be and they are hereby appointed Overseers to open and Keep the Same in repair.

Ordered, that there be a publick ferry established across Savannah River, landing at the mouth of Cold Water Creek, on the Site whereon the Ware house is to be established.

Jason Wilson }
vs } Case
John Parker & }
Daniel Parker }

Dismised.

November the 15th 1797

Present, his honor Judge Higginbotham

Jurors drawn for the Next Term, to wit.

1. [illegible] Penn
2. John Brown
3. [illegible] Stricklin
4. David [illegible]
5. Nathan Smith
6. Buford Doss
7. John Smith
8. Barnard Kelly
9. Mose Bell
10. Dionysius Oliver
11. William [illegible]
12. William Blake
13. David Head
14. Robert Ewing
15. Thomas McAlpin
16. Benjamin Kelley
17. John McClary
18. [illegible] Dale
19. James Griffith
20. Joseph Sewell
21. Hardin Evans
22. Forester Upshaw
25. Wm Post
26. James Butler
27. [illegible]
28. John Patterson
29. James Brown
30. Andrew Cunningham
31. Josiah Sartain
32. John Spears
33. John McKinsey
34. Alexander Thompson
35. Robert Griffith
36. George [illegible]
37. Robert Black
38. James Huff
39. John Pollard
40. John Hawsey
41. Stephen Allinton
42. John Cloud
43. Caleb Oliver
44. Middleton Faning
45. John Lowry
46. Loftin [illegible]

23. Darvin Harris	47. Philip Lewis
24. James Alexander	48. Walker Richardson

At an Inferior Court held at Elbert Courthouse the 19th day of December 1797. [82]

Present, William Barnett, Richardson Hunt, Sam[l] Higginbotham, Ralp Banks, Reuben Allen, Esquires

On the Petition of Eli Eavenson, praying that he might obtain a Licence to keep a Tavern at Elbert Court House.

Ordered, that the Same be granted, on the said Eavensons giving bond, as the Law directs in Such Cases.

Harris & Carter }
vs } Case
Robert Buckner }

I do Confess Judgment in the within Case, for seventy four dollars and Twelve and a half Cents, with Interest, from the first June 1797.

Test. M. Williamson
Dec[r] 19th 1797

Robert Buckner

On the Petition of Thomas B. Creagh, Praying that William Jones be bound to him.

Ordered, that the Same be granted, upon the compliance of said Tho[s] B. Creagh with the requisits of the Law in that Case.

When Thomas B. Creagh and Thomas Burton came into Court and acknowledged themselves bound unto the Justices of the Inferior Court of Elbert County and their Successors in office, in the Sum of Five Hundred Dollars, to be Void on Conditions, that the said Thomas B. Creagh does Learn or use this Endeavor to Learn William Jones the Trade, Art, or Mistery of Tayler, and furnish him with holsom Meat, Lodging, and Clothes, during the time for which he is bound, and give him eighteen Months Schooling, and when the Said Jones Arrives to age of twenty one to furnish him, the said Jones, with the Tools sufficient to Carry on said trade.

T. B. Creagh, Thom. Burton

John M. Whitney }
vs } Case
Elisha Brewer & }
Samuel Black } [83]

Jury Sworn (to wit)

1. Darbin Harris
2. Nath[l] Smith
3. James Huff
4. John Brown
5. And[w] Cunningham
6. James Buttler
7. Jisiah Sartain
8. James Brown
9. Walk[r] Richardson
10. Stephen Allington
11. Middlin Faning
12. Absalom Davis

The Jury returned, and the Plaintiff, being three times Called, and Not answering, a Nonsuit ordered.

John Henly }
vs } Case
Robert Buckner }

I do Confess Judgment in this case, for Ninety dollars and fifty six Cents, with Interest from the 17th July 1797 & Costs.

Robert Buckner

Test. M. W[m]son

Dec[r] 19th 1797

Harriss & Carter }
vs } Assumsit
James Wright }

I Do Confess Judgment, in the within Case, for Eighty one dollars, Nine & three quarter Cents, with Costs, with Stay of Execution forty days.

Test. M. W[m]son James Wright
Dec[r] 19th 1797

J. Kidd }
vs } Continuance
R^{n} Frazure }

On application of William Thompson, Jr,

Ordered, that he be appointed Guardian for Tabitha Thompson, upon his Complying with the Requisits of the law in that Case.

A petition from Thomas Meriwether praying that the ford on Broad River Called Brinells ford, Might be Kept open was read.

Ordered, that Thomas B. Scott and Joseph Deadwiler be appointed Commissioner to view Said ford and make their report to the Next Court.

The Court then adjourned till tomorrow ten O'clock.

Wm Barnett, R. Hunt, R. Banks. Reubin Allen

Wednesday, the 20th [84]

The Court met agreeable to adjournment.

Present, their Honors William Barnett, R. Hunt, Higginbotham, Banks, & Allen

James Shockly }
vs }
Elij^{h} Owens & Co }

Continuance by Consent made a preemptory risk for trial the Next Term.

James Shockly }
vs }
Stephen Haynes & Co }

Continuance by Consent made a preemptory risk for trial at the Next Term.

Trion Harriss }
vs } Trover
W^{m} McDowell}

First Trial waved and Apeal by Consent without Security. The Cost to follow the event of the Verdict on the appeal.

Early, for Pltff.
Carnes, for Def[t]
20th Dec[r] 1797

M. Woods }
vs }
William Carter }

Jury Sworn (to wit)

1. Andrew Cuningham	7. John Brown
2. James Griffith	8. Harden Evans
3. Darvin Harriss	9. Midleton Faning
4. Josiah Sartain	10. Peter Johnson
5. Rich[d] Ross	11. Stephen Alington
6. James Huff	12. Wak[r] Richardson

We find for the Plaintiff ferty Nine Dollars, Six & half Cents.

W. Richardson

Josiah Sartain }
vs }
W[m] Elliott }

Jury N[o] 1 Sworn.

We find for the Plaintiff One Hundred and Six dollars & Costs.

Walker Richardson

James Thurmon }
vs }
J. H. Johnson }
et al }

The Plaintiff being Three times Called, and Not answering, Ordered A. Nonsuit.

Ch[s] W[m]son }
vs } Case
J. M. Whitney } [85]

Jury N[o] 1 Sworn.

We the Jury find for the Plaintiff for Ninety six dollars & a half, with Interest, from the Twelfth day of December 1797.

Walk Richardson

William Goode Assinee }
of W[m] Hatcher }
vs }
Evan Ragland }

Setled.

W[m] Aycock }
for C. Easter }
vs }
Rob[t] Moon & wife }

Continued.

Leroy Pope }
vs } Case
Joseph Huddleston }

Jury N[o] 1 Sworn.

We the Jury find for the Plaintiff fifty seven dollars & forty three Cents & Costs.

W. Richardson

W[m] Chislom }
vs } Case
Jn[o] M. Whitney }

We find for the Plaintiff One hundred and Eleven Dollars & fifty Cents.

Walker Richardson

Upon the petition of the Rev[d] John Andrew, Stating that he has a brother, Thomas Andrew, who is not in a Situation to Conduct his own Private Conserns, and that he is Possessed of a Considerable Property, whereupon the Court appointed the said John Andrew Guardian for the Said Th[s] Andrew, he Gives Security in the Sum of $2000.

Eldredge Hargrove }
vs } Case
Jn° M. Whitney }

Jury N° 1 Sworn.

We the Jury find for the Plaintiff Twelve Hundred and fifty dollars, which may be discharged be making a good and Sufficient Right & Title to the within Mentioned Land in four months.

Walker Richardson

On Motion, Ordered, that Drury Bradly be appointed Guardian for Francis Greenwood, miner, he Complying with the Requisits of Law in that case.

Wm Brawner }
vs }
F. Upshaw }

Settled.

Ferdinand Phinizy } [86]
vs } Debt
John Doss }

I Do hereby Confess Judgment to the Plaintiff for the Sum of Two hundred and Thirty two dollars, forty Two and Two Thirds Cents, with Interest and Costs, Stay of Execution twelve months from this day, provided I give Security with in Twenty days. Daniel White entered Security.

John Doss

William Meredith }
vs } Debt
Leroy Pope }

Jury N° 1 Sworn.

We the Jury find for the Plaintiff One hundred and fifty three dollars, with Cost.

Walker Richardson

Jacob Carter }
vs } Case
Charles Goss }

I do hereby Confess Judgment for the Sum of One hundred and thirty five dollars, with Interest from the Twenty fourth of December 1796. Execution Stayed till April next.

Ch[s] Goss

J. Mathews

Henry Coldwell for }
the use of Geo. Kaning }
vs } Case
Administrators of }
Edm[d] Bauer }

Jury N[o] 1 Sworn.

We the Jury find for the Plaintiff One hundred and four dollars, & Costs.

Walker Richardson

John Wilson }
vs } Case
J. M. Whitney }

Jury N[o] 1 Sworn.

We the Jury find for the Plaintiff four hundred and Twenty dollars and thirty Cents, with Interest agreeable to the date of the Order.

Walker Richardson

Ordered, that James Christian be appointed Overseer of that Part of the Road from Larkin Gatewoods to Robert Shepperds, and Turner Christian from thence to Francis Baties ~~old Place and land~~, James Lawson from thence to Cancellers old place, and Samuel Akins from thence to the old road above Fairgus Creek.

Ordered, that Cristopher Clark be appointed Overseer from the fishdam Road, down the River to Elisha Brewers.

Ordered, that there be a road laid out, from the Oglethorpe line at David Ewings Saw Mill, [87] to the line Shoal on North fork of Broad River, and that John McKee, Samuel Nelson, and David Ewing be appointed Commissioners to View and report to the next Inferior Court, the Best and Most Convenient way for said road to run.

Ordered, that Robert Tait be appointed overseer of that Part of the Road, from James Alstons ford on the Beaverdam, to E. Towns, and Richard Colbert from Alstons ford to Vanns Creek, and John Moon from thence to McGarrys ford Cold Water.

The Court then adjourned untill Court in Course.

Test. M. Woods   Wm Barnett, R. Hunt, R. Banks, R. Allen

—

At an Inferior Court begun and held at Elberton, the 19th day of July 1798.

Present, Wm Barnett, Richardson Hunt, Saml Higginbotham, Ralph Banks, Reuben Allen

John M. Whitney }
vs } Debt
E. Brewer & }
M. J. Williams }

Dismist at the defendants Cost.

James Shockley }
vs } Assault
Elijah Owens & }
Benjamin Howard }

Jury Sworn, to wit.

1. James Brock	7. Andrew Walker
2. Joshua McConnell	8. George Averhart
3. Wm Brown	9. John Algood
4. Thomas Jones	10. Andrew Brown
5. Nathl Etchison	11. Zachariah Clark
6. Alexander Human	12. John Calvert

The Jury being Called and one failing to answer, the Same was Ordered to be a Nonsuit.

James Shokley } [88]
vs }
Stephen Haynes }
et al }

Nonsuit.

John Henly } vs } Case Robert Buckner }		Harris & Carter } vs } case Robert Buckner }	

In those Cases of Special Bail, Jacob Dyer, the Special Bail in these Cases, came into Court and Surrendered the Body of the Principal, Robert Buckner. Wherefore, it is Ordered, the said Robert Buckner be in the Custody of the Sheriff, and that the Bail be discharged from his recognizance.

resolved, that it be Considered hereafter as a Standing Rule of this Court, Whenever a point is made by any Gentleman of the Bar, On which a decision of this Court is required, the Judges on the Bench Shall Give their Opinion Seriatim, one by one, the Justice presiding Shall ask the Youngest Judge his opinion first, and so on, untill the opinion of the Court is Taken, which Shall be pronounced by the Presiding Judge. Also, it is Ordered, that no one Gentleman of the Bar be permited to Speak to any Motion or Legal point made to this Court more than Once, except the Council Moving the Point, who Shall have the priviledge of Conclusion.

On the petition Robert L. Tait.

Ordered, that his Tavern Licence be renewed, on his Complying with the requisits of the Law.

On the petition of John Sanders Walker'

Ordered, that Memorable Walker be appointed his Guardian, on his Complying with the law in Such Cases.

On Motion of Mr Griffin.

It is Ordered, that Samuel Fuller, an Orphan, be Bound unto Thomas Napier, he entering into bond and Security, to Give the Orphan One years Schooling, and maintain him with Suitable Clothing & Diet, and use his endeavours to Learn him the Brick Layers Trade.

I, Robert Middleton, high Sheriff, of the County of Elbert and State of Georgia, do hereby, in Open Court, before their honors, the Justices of said Court, protest against the Sufficiency and Safety of the Publick Jail of said County, as not being Adequate for the detention of any prisoner, and do hereby declare that I will not Consider for myself for any escapes therefrom.

Signed in Open Court, Robert Middleton, Shff
this 19th July 1798

Ordered, that Joseph Pulliam, Thomas Penn, N. Bonds, John Beard, Reuben Cook, Nathaniel Williford, Robert Moon, ~~John~~ Wm Brawner, Thomas Akin, & Leroy Paice be and they are hereby appointed Constables, for the present year, on their Complying with the Law in Such Cases made and provided.

On Petition of Sam[l] Higginbotham, Esqr.

Ordered, that he Obtain tavern Licence to retail Spirituous Liquors&c, at his own Mill, on his Giving bond and Complying with the Law in Such Cases Made & Provided. [89]

Ordered, that Joseph Deadwilder be and he is hereby appointed Overseer to open a Road from Barnetts old ford on Broad River, the Most Direct way leading to Elbert Court House, and to make the Bank of said River passable, and to Keep the same in Good Order.

Court then Adjourned, untill tomorrow ten O'clock.

M. Woods

Fryday, 20th July 1798

Present, as yesterday.

On Motion, in behalf of Sarah Akin & Thomas Akin, Administrators of the Estate of Joseph Akin, Dec[d], praying that the real Estate of said Joseph Akin, to wit. Two hundred acres of Land, adjoining the Lands of Drury Thompson & James F. Nunnalee, Should be Sold for the Benefit of the heirs & the Representatives of the said

---

Joseph, and it appearing Satisfactory to this Court that Notice had been duly given according to Law, it also appearing that it would be for the Benefit of the Heirs &c, of the said Joseph Akin, that the Said tract of Land Should be Sold, and, it is therefore, Ordered, that the said Tract of land be Sold & Disposed of, According to the Act in Such Cases made and provided.

James Gates, Admr }
of S. Eperson, Decd }
vs } Case
Elisha Johnson & }
John H. Johnson }

Jury Sworn, to wit.

1. Andrew Walker	7. Zachariah Clark
2. Alexander Human	8. W[m] Hatcher
3. Thomas Jones	9. W. Blankingship
4. Joshua McConnell	10. John Allgood

5. James Brock | 11. Nath[l] Etcherson
6. William Brown | 12. Thomas Oliver

We find for the Plaintiff Sixty six dollars and thirty seven & ½ Cents, with Interest and Cost.

W[m] Brown, foreman

Harry Colwell for }
use George Haning }
vs } Case
Thomas Burton }

Jury as in the above Case.

We the Jury find for the Plaintiff ninety nine dollars and ninety four Cents, with Cost of Suit.

W[m] Brown, Foreman

Farley Thompson } [90]
vs } Case
Evan Ragland }

Jury Sworn, to wit, N[o] 2.

1. Thomas Napier	7. Martin Turman
2.Thomas Woodridge	8. Thomas Cook
3. Joseph Bell	9. Joseph Long
4. Walter Nunnalee	10. Adam Garr
5. J. W. Cuningham	11. Benjamin Brown
6. John Carrell	12. W[m] Howington

We the Jury find for the defendant ten dollars.

Jn[o] Cuningham, F. M.

The Court Proceeded to appoint One fit and proper person in Each Battalion to take the Sensus or Enumeration of all free White Persons and people of Colour Residing therein, And after Comparing their Ballots, it appeared that Nathaniel Alston, Esq[r] was duly Elected for the Lower battalion, Absalom Stinchcomb, Esq[r] for the Middle, & Francis Cook, Esquire for the upper.

S. Stokes }
vs }
J. Kidd }

I, James Kidd, the Defendant, and Charter Harper, the Security, do acknowledge ourselves Jointly and Severly Bound unto the plaintiff in the Sum Mentioned in the Sheriffs bond, Conditioned that, if the defendant Gets Cast in this Suit, that he will pay the Condemnation money, or Surrender himself as the Law directs, or I will do it for him. Taken and acknowledged in Open Court.

James Kidd, Charter Harper

M. Woods }
vs } Case
John Depriest }

We, John Depriest and Henry Gatewood, do acknowledge Ourselves Indebted to Plaintiff double the Sum Insuited in the Sheriffs Bond, Conditioned that if the Defendant does not pay the Condemnation money or Surrender himself as the Law directs that I will do it for him.

John Priest, H. Gatewood

Wm Thompson }
vs } Case
J. Morrison & }
James Morrison }

Judgment Confest for forty dollars and ninety Eight Cents, with Interest from the 3 day of August 1792, with Stay of Execution till first day January next.

James Morrison

On the Petition of Thomas Tait.

Ordered, that he Obtain Tavern Licence, by his Compliance of the Law, in that Case &c.

The Court proceeded to appoint Inspectors for the upper & Lower Warehouse in Petersburg. Thomas Burton, J^{r}, Charles Taylor, & Robert Watkins be and they are hereby appointed Inspectors of Tobacco for the Lower, or Olivers, ware house in Petersburg.

Thomas Burton, Senr, Wm Reynolds, and William Hatcher be and they are hereby [91]
appointed Inspectors of Tobacco for the upper, or Watkinses, Ware House in Petersburg.

Wm Aycock, guardian }
of C. Easter }
vs } Special action on the Case
Robert Moore & wife }

Dismist, at the Plaintiffs Cost.

Leroy Pope }
vs } Case
Charles Hudson }

Judgment Confest for $96.87 Cents, with Stay of Execution till the 1st April next.

C. Tait, Deft. Atty.

Leroy Pope }
vs } Case
Chs Hudson & }
Wm Hudson }

Judgment Confest for $96.38 Cents, with Stay of Execution till the 1st April next.

C. Tait, Deft. Atty.

On William Hatchers Signifying to the Court his nonacceptance to the appointment of Inspector for the upper warehouse. It is Ordered, that George Turman be and he is hereby appointed Inspector in Lieu there of.

Nathaniel Hudson, Administrator of David Hudson, Decd, and Thomas Oliver, having refered Controversy to the final Decision of Charles Tait and Absalom Stinch Comb, Esquires, do make their award and have Returned the Same to this Court in the words following, to wit.

We, the Arbitrators, to whom was refered the Matters in dispute Between Thomas Oliver and the Heirs and Representatives of David Hudson, are of Opinion that Thomas Oliver shall make good and Sufficient titles to half of a tract of Land, granted to John Blake, Containing Ninety and an half acres and that the Heirs and Representatives of David Hudson pay to the said Thomas Oliver One Hundred and forty two dollars, Sixty Eight & ¾ Cents. April 19th 1798.

Chs Tait
A. Stinchcomb

Ordered, that Edmund Shackleford be appointed Overseer of the Road from his ferry to I. Settles & William Gibbs, from thence to Francis Cooks.

Ordered, that Thomas Duglass be appointed Overseer of that part of the Savannah Petersburg Road, from Elisha Townses to Edward Walthalls.

Ordered, that Thomas Carter, J^r be appointed Overseer of that part of Road, Leading from Elbret Court House, to Col^o Higginbothams Ford on the Beaverdam Creek, Joshua Underwood from the said ford to Cold Water Creek at Tyners ford, James Jones from the said ford to the Bridge on Little Cold Water, at the said Joneses Plantation, Samuel Self from the Said Bridge to Hugh McDonalds, Esquires. [92]

Hugh McDonald}
vs } Case
Francis Powell }

Suit Settled.

Hugh McDonald}
vs } Case
Francis Powell }

Suit Settled.

John Hawthorn }
vs } Case
Fleming Greenwood }
Surviving Promiser of }
John & Fleming Greenwood }

Settled.

The Court then adjourned till Court in Course.

Test. M. Woods — Wm Barnett, R. Banks, R. Allen, R. Hunt, Sam Higginbotham

---

At an Inferior Court held at Elberton, this 19th day of December 1798.

Present, William Barnett, R. Hunt, Reuben Allen, Ralph Banks, & Saml Higginbotham, Esquires

William Diggs }
vs } Case
John Martin }

Jury Sworn, to wit.

1. Leonard Rice	7. Adley Alexander
2. John Cook	8. Luke Hambleton
3. Samuel Baker	9. James F. Nunnelee
4. William Teasley	10. John Kees
5. John Murry	11. Jacob Odem
6. John Davis	12. Darben Harris

We the Jury find for the plaintiff Two hundred & Seventy two Dollars, forty Seven cents.

James F. Nunnelee

Stephen Heard }
vs } Covenant
Nath[l] Evans }
Henry Burton & }
Charles Hudson }

Jury Sworn, to wit.

1. Sherod Harris	7. Sylvanus Stokes
2. Daniel Johnson	8. John King
3. Sam[l] Paxton	9. Thomas Oliver
4. Robert Laremore	10. Isham Morgan
5. John Chambers	11. John Moon
6. John Dingler	12. A. Higginbotham

We the Jury find for the plaintiff two hundred and twenty one dollars.

Tho[s] Oliver, For[n]

Silvanus Stokes } [93]
vs }
James Kidd }

the Same Jury as in the Case Diggs vs Martin.

We the Jury find for the plaintiff One hundred and Ninety Eight dollars, Seventy two Cents.

James F. Nunnelee

Thomas Woldridge in }
right of his wife Keziah }
vs } Special Case
Absalom Davis }
& Others }

We, Absalom Davis, Jun[r], Joseph Davis, and Gideon Davis, the defendants, and John Coleman, the Security, do Acknowledge ourselves Justly indebted to the Plaintiffs in Double the Sum Mentioned in the Sheriffs Bond. To be Void on this Condition, that if we, the Defendants, Shall be cast in the above Suit, that will pay the Condemnation Money, or Surrender ourselves in Court as the Law directs, or I, as Security, will do it for them. Taken and acknowledged in Court.

Gideon Davis, Joseph Davis, Absalom Davis,
John Coleman

Ordered, that Tryon Harris be appointed Guardian for Sally Thompson, his complying with the Law.

Benjamin Cook }
vs }
Gerrard Walthall }

I, Gerrard Walthall, Jun[r], the defendant, and Gerald Wathall, Sen[r], the Security, do acknowledge ourselves indebted to the plaintiff in double the Sum Mentioned in the Sheriffs Bond, Conditioned that if the defendant Shall be cast in the above Suit, that I, the defendant, will pay the Condemnation Money, or Surrender Myself in Court as the Law directs, or I will do it for him. Taken and acknowledged in Open Court.

G. Walthall, Gerrard Walthall

Middleton Woods }
vs }
John Depriest }

The Same Jury as in the Case Heard vs Evans, et al.

We the Jury find for the plaintiff Sixty Three dollars and fifty Six Cents.

Thomas Oliver

Leroy Pope for }
George Cook }
vs }
Christopher Harris}

The Same Jury as in the Case Diggs vs Martin.

We the Jury find for the plaintiff Sixty three dollars and Seventy two Cents.

James F. Nunnelee

Susannah Colbert }
vs }
A. Bell & E. Towns }

put out for miscalling the names.

James Shepperd } [94]
vs }
John Cook }

I confess Judgment on the within Suit for one Hundred and Ninety Two dollars.

John Cook

Leroy Pope }
vs }
Sherod Harris }

The Bail below, Tryon Harris, with the defendant, came into Court and acknowledged themselves bound unto the Plaintiff in double the Sum Mentioned in the Sheriffs bond, On this Condition, that if the defendant Shall be cast in the above Suit, that he, the defendant, will pay the Condemnation Money, or Surrender himself as the law directs, or I will do it for him.

Sherwood Harris, Tryon Harris

Jonathan Tair }
vs }
Peter Johnson }
et al }

We, Angus Johnson, As[d] Johnson, John McDonald, James Brown, Jun[r], & Daniel Johnson, M. Johnson, John McDaniel, Ju[r], W[m] McKenzie, & A. McDonald, Defendants, and we, R. T. Cosby, Donald McDonald, John King, Donald McDonald, Sen[r], James Brown, R. McDonald, the Securities, do acknowledge ourselves indebted to the plaintiff in double

—

double the Sum Mentioned in the Sheriffs bond, on this Condition, that if the defendant Should be cast, that we will pay the Condition Money, or Surrender ourselves as the Law directs, or we will do it for him.

Daniel Johnson, A. McDonald, John McDonald,
A. Johnson, James Brown, MKenzie,
John McDonald, R. T. Cosby, John King,
Donald McDonald, Donald McDonald,
Roderick McDonald, James Brown

David Witt }
vs } Case
John M. Whitney }

In this Case, Moses Payne and Robert Kennedy came into Court and acknowledged themselves Special Bail upon the usual Terms.

Benajah Smith }
vs } attachment
Edward Watts }

In this case, it appearing by the return of the Sheriff that a horse was leved on by virtue of the above Attachment on the property of Edward Watts and not being replevied. It is Ordered, that the Same be Sold in terms of the Law in Such case made and provided, & that the money arising on Said Sale be deposited in the Clerks office, Subject to the future direction

of the Court. [95]

Ordered, that there be a ferry established a Cross Broad River at Edward Denny's plantation.

Ordered, that Thomas Oliver, John R. Ragland, James Coleman, James O. Cosby, and Reuben Lindsay do obtain Tavern Licence to retail Spirituous liquors &c, at their respecting dwelling houses, for and during the Term of One year, with their Complying with the Law in Such Cases.

The Court proceeded to appoint Inspectors for Middleton's Ware House, Mouth of Cold Water, when William Alexander, Henry Harper, and John Carson Was appointed.

Jurors drawn for the next term.

1. James Jarmany
2. James Sutton
3. John Hamm
4. Hardin Evan
5. James Hawthorn
6. Jonathan Lane
7. Edward Lowry
8. John Banks
9. Robert Tait
10. Vanatine Smith
11. Caleb Oliver
12. William Dodd
13. Benjamin Davis
14. George Henderson

---

15. William Head
16. Jeremiah Walker
17. James McDonall
18. Robert Smith
19. William Pickins
20. Charles Parks
21. John Royall
22. Benjamin Higganbotham
23. Peter Shepherd
24. John Heard
25. William Hay
26. William Suttle
27. William Carter
28. Peter Tidwell
29. James McGowan
30. Obediah Finney
31. Joseph King
32. James Rogers
33. James Huff
34. Solomon Strickland
35. Elisha Towns
36. Alexander Thompson
37. Richard Woods
38. William Hodge
39. Hugh McDonall
40. Stephen Stephens
41. James Glover
42. John Darden
43. Arthur Jones
44. William Cawthon
45. George Alexander
46. John Brown, Senr
47. John Lowry
48. John Parker
49. David Roberson
50. David Franklin
51. Henry Jackson
52. Joseph Blackwell
53. George Wych
54. Gidean Davis

Court then is adjourned till Court in Course.

William Barnett, Richardson Hunt, Ralph Banks, Reuben Allen, Samuel Higganbotham

At an Inferior Court held at Elberton the 19th day of July 1799. [96]

Present, Wm Barnett, R. Hunt, R. Banks, S. Higginbotham, R. Allen, Esquires

Howell Cobbs }
vs }
Edward Watts }

In this case, it appearing to the Court that a Judgt was obtained by the Plaintiff against the defendant in the County of Burk, on the third day of September 1798, and that an Execution Hath issued thereon, which is now in the hands of the Sheriff of this County, & it also appearing that there are in the hands of said Sheriff Sixty six dollars, being the overplus of property sold under under a Mortgage to satisfy Wm Bibbs and also others, money arising out of the sale of perishable property sold under an Attachmentin behalf of Benajor Smith, both which sums of money are the property of said Watts. On motion.

It is Ordered, that the Sheriff shew cause Tomorrow morning at ten O'Clock, why the money aforesaid shall not be paid over to satisfy the Execution aforesaid in behalf of said Cobbs.

James Kidd }
vs } Con^d^
Reuben Frazer }

John Morrow }
vs }
Thompson McGuire }
& A. McGuire }

Jury Sworn, to wit.

1. Wm Carter
2. Robert L. Tate
3. James Sutton
4. Robert Smith
5. Edwd Lowry
6. Caleb Oliver
7. James Glover
8. James Jarvis
9. Wm Hodge
10. Wm Cothorn
11. Elisha Towns
12. James McDonald

We the Jury find the plaintiff $222.36½, with Cost of Suit.

Robt L. Tait

L. Walker, J. Carter }
& H. Graves Walker }
vs }
Thomas Carter }

Continued by the defendant, affidavit and all exceptions Waved.

Henry C[smear]bell }
Guardian for Gilbert Chaves }
vs } Ass[t] & battery
Thompson Bird }
et al }

Jury Sworn, to wit.

1. Mathew J. Williams	7. John Hames
2. Robert Martin	8. Thomas Patterson
3. James Huff	9. Henry Grave Walker
4. George Wych	10. Thomas Burton
5. W[m] Chisolm	11. James Kidd
6. David Franklin	12. Francis Higginbotham

[97]

We the Jury do find for the Plaintiff thirty one dollars & Cost. Thomas Munger excepted.

M. J. Williams, For[n]

Peter Wych acknowledged himself Sec[y].

George Cook & E. Cook }
vs }
Tryon Harris & C. Harris }

Continued, on the affidavit of the Defendant, and all exceptions Waved.

Geo. & E. Cook }
vs }
Tryon & D. Harris }

Geo. & E. Cook }
vs }
Tryon & D. Harris }

Con[d], as above.

Manus Limly }
vs }
James Crow }

Cont[d], on the affidavit of the Defendant.

Richard George }
vs }
River Jourdon }

John Morrow, the Common Bail, surrendered his principal into Court. When River Jourdon, the defendant, and Over River Jourdon & Joshua Jourdon, The securities, do acknowledge ourselves bound unto the plaintiff in Double the sum mentioned in the Sheriff Bail bond, on this condition, that if the Defendant Should be cast, that he would pay the Condemnation money, or surrender himself as the Law Directs, , Or we will do it for him. Acknowledged

---

in Court.

River X Jourdon his mark
Over R. Jourdon, Joshua Jourdon,
M. Woods Jn° Middleton

The Court then adjourned till tomorrow ten O'Clock.

Wm Barnett, R. Allen, R. Hunt, S. Higginbotham

Saturday, 20th July 1799

The Court met pursuant to adjournment.

Present, Wm Barnett, R. Hunt, R. Banks, R. Allen, S. Higginbotham, Esquires

Howell Cobbs }
vs }
Edward Watts }

in this Case, a Rule having been obtained against the Sheriff to Shew Cause why Certain monies in his hand belong to the Defendant Should not be paid over in satisfaction of an execution on behalf of the plaintiff & no Cause being Shown, it is ordered by the Court that the Sheriff pay over toward Satisfying Said Execution the sum of one hundred and six dollars out of the monies So in his hands.

Woods & Lindsay } [97]
vs }
David Nelms }

David Nelms, the defendant, and Rowland Brown, the Security, DO acknowledge our selves bound to the Plaintiff in Double the Sum mentioned in Sheriffs Bail Bond, to be Void on this

Condition, that if the defendant be cast, that he will pay the Condemnation Money, or Surrender himself as the Law directs, or I will do it for him. Acknowledged in Court.

David Nelms, Rowland X Brown his mark

Benajah Smith }
vs } Attachment
Edward Watts }

The same Jury as in the Case Morrow vs McGuire.

We the Juryers find for the Plantiff seven hundred seventy seven dollars, twenty five Cents.

R. L. Tait

Le Roy Pope }
vs } Case
Sherod Harris }

Jury Sworn, to wit.

1. Wm Carter	7. James Glover
2. Robert L. Tait	8. George Wych
3. James Sutton	9. William Hodge
4. Robert Smith	10. Wm Cawthorn
5. James Huff	11. Ilisha Towne
6. Caleb Oliver	12. Jamees McDonland

We the Juryers find for the plaintiff fifty four Dollars twelve Cents, with Cost.

Robert L. Tate

Eli Williams }
vs }
Leroy Upshaw }

The same Jury as ~~with~~ in the above Case.

We the Jury find for the Plaintiff 56.35½ with Cost.

Robt L. Tait

John Semples acknowledged himself Sec^{y}.

John Griffin }
vs }
Hugh McDonald }
John Murrah }

The Jury as above.

We the Jury find for the Plaintiff 165.71½ with Cost.

Rob[t] L. Tait

Sam[l] Philips }
vs }
Jacob Odem }

The same Jureyers find Judg[t] for the Defendant.

Rob[t] L. Tait

John Hurt }
vs } Case Bail
William Winn }

William Winn, the Deft, and Richmond Cosby, as Bail, Came into Acknowledged them selves bound to the plaintiff in double the sum mentioned Conditioned in the bail bond, to be Void on the condition, that if the Defendant be cast, he will pay the Condemnation Money, or surrender himself as the law directs, or I will do it for him. Acknowledged in Open Court.

W[m] Winn, R. T. Cosby

Mary Phair } [98]
vs }
Jonathan Phair }

The bail brought the Defendant into Court & surrendered him.

Mary Phair }
vs } Case
Jonathan Phair } Ball

Jonathan Phair Comes into Court & offers Special Bail, Samuel Self, who Acknowledges himself bound to the plaintiff in double the sum mentioned in the bail bond, upon this Condition, that if the Defendant be Cast, he will pay the Condemnation Money, or surrender himself as the law directs, or I will do it for him. Acknowledged in Open Court.

J. Phair, Samuel Self

John Hurbbard}
vs } Case
Eli Eaverson }

I do Confess Judgement for the sum of one hundred & Eighty two & eighty four & one Quarter Cents, with interest from the third day of November 1798, and stay of Execution six months.

Eli Everson

Robert Thompson & Walkrires }
vs } Case Bail
John Algood }

John Algood came into Court & offered David Nelms as Special bale, Who Acknowledged himself bound to the plantiff in double

---

Double the sum specified in the bail bond, upon this Condition, that if the defendant be cast, he will pay the Condemnation Money, or Surrender himself as the law Directs, or I will pay it for him. Acknowledged in open Court.

John X Algood his mark
David Nelms

Robert L. Tait }
vs } Attachment
Robert Martine }

dismissed.

The Court perceeded to the appointment of Inspectors, when it appeared that Thomas Burton, Junr, & Charles Taylor for first Inspectors, Robert Burton as third Inspector, and John Sharp picker, was duly appointed for Olivers Ware house. Joel Crawford and Francis Satterwhite as first Inspectors, William Watkins as third Inspector, and Francis Higginbotham Picker was Duly Appointed for Watkins Warehouse. Henry Harper and John Carson as first Inspectors, Wm Alexander as third Inspector, and George Rucker as picker, for cold Water Ware House. Edmond Shakaford and John Blake as first Inspectors & John Wilhite third Inspector, and Thomas Posey as picker, for Easters Ware House.

Woods & Lindsay }
vs }
Gabriel Higginbotham } [99]

Gabriel Higginbotham, the defendant, and Caleb Higginbotham, the Sec^{y}, do Acknowledge Our selves bound unto plaintiff in double the sum Mentioned in the Bale bond, Conditioned, that if the defendant should be Cast on the above Suit, that he, the defendant, will pay the Condemnation Money, or surrender himself as the law Directs, or I will do it for him. Acknowledged in Court.

M. Woods

Gabriel Higginbotham
Caleb Higginbotham

James Kidd }
vs }
John Greenwood }

James B. Floyd }
& James Kidd }
vs }
John Greenwood }

It appearing to the Court, that a bound for referring the above Causes was deposited with David Webb for safe Keeping.

Ordered, that the said David Shew Cause, if Any he has, at the next term, Why he does not produce the same to the Court.

Upon Motion of Mr Griffin, Stating to the Court, that Absalom Davis, Senr as a material witness in the Case Gideon Davis vs Thomas Wooldridge & Thomas Wooldridge vs Absalom Davis, Junr, in the first Case

---

For Plaintiff, and in the second for the defendant, and it appearing to the Satisfaction to the Court upon Oath, that the said Absalom Davis, Senr is old and infirm, and in all probability will not live untill the next term.

It is Ordered, that a Rule be Granted, take the examination of the said Absalom Davis, upon Interrogatories de bene esse, the said agent giving the adverse party, Thomas Wooldridge, or his attorney, at Least ten days Notice of the day on which such examination is to be taken, the Competency of such Evidence To be in the power of the Court.

Benj. Smith }
vs } Attachment
Edward Watts }

In this Case, by the Return of the Sheriff, it appearing that one horse had been livered, and the same sold for seventy dollars, as p[r] Return of the Sheriff. On the Order of the Court for the Sale thereof, and an Elder Execution and Judgment Claiming forty Dollars of the said sum. Ordered, that the balance of thirty Dollars be paid to the plantiff or his Att[y], he having established his Demand against the Defendant.

Elias Alexander }
vs } attachment
John Ross }

Dismias.

Alexander Blair, Att[y] } [100]
for William Waugh }
vs } att[t]
William Stephens }

Dismmised.

Susannah Colbert }
vs }
Abraham Bell & }
Elisha Towns }

Settled.

Thadias Holt }
vs }
William Cox & }
Stephen Heard }

Settled.

Thomas Lovelady }
vs }
Jacob Odem }

Setled.

Le Roy Pope }
vs }
Mathias Williamson }

settled.

On the petition of James Brady, praying that that a Guardian be appointed for William Brazel, Minor. Ordered, that James Glover be Appointed as such, he Complying with the law in such Cases.

The Court then Adjourned untill Monday, ten O'Clock.

Wm Barnett, R. Allen, R. Hunt, S. Higginbotham

Monday, 22nd July 1799

The Court met Pursuant to Adjournment.

Present, Wm Barnett, R. Hunt, Ralph Banks, R. Allen, S. Higginbotham, Esq^rs

On Motion of Mr Tait.

It is Ordered, that A note of hand or bond on which a Recovery has been had vs Wamack Blankenship in the Case as indorsee of said Note or bond at the Instance of John Heard be given up to the Womack Blankenship Judgment being Written in the fill of it.

Agreeable to the Recommendation of the Grand Jury, It is Ordered, that Saml Post have a ferry established at Broad River on his Own land.

On the Petition, Jeremiah Walker, James Kidd, and Pleasant Statham, praying that they might Keep a house of Entertainment, and be permited to Retail Spirituous Liquors &c, at their Respective Dweling houses.

Ordered, that the same be granted, on their Complying with the Requisits of the Law.

Robert Thompson } [101]
vs }
Robert Singleton }

I, Robert Singleton, the Defendant, and William Dudly, John Depriest, Isaac D. Manley, & Thomas Lovelady, the Sec^ys, Acknowledge ourselves bound unto The Plaintiff in double the sum Mentioned in the Sheriff Bail bond, to be Void on Conditions, that if the defendant shall be cast, that he will pay the condemnation money, or surrender himself as the Law directs, or we will do it for him. Acknowledged in Court.

Robert Singleton, Wm Dudley, John Depriest,
Isaac D. Manley, Thos Lovelatty

Ordered, that Anguss Johnson be allowed to draw ten Dollars, out of any moneyes now in the Possession of the Clark, and appropriate the same to the use of Alexander McDonald, a poor person.

Also Ordered, that Absalom Stinchcomb be allowed to draw Eight dollars out of any money now in the Clarks hands, and appropriate the same to the use of the Widow Cane and her daughter Nancy McKee.

Ordered, that James Stroud & John Stroud, children of Milly Stroud ~~to~~ be bound unto Reuben Satterwhite, in terms of the Law in that case made and provided, and that said Satterwhite give said boys two years Schooling.

Ordered, that John Staples, Wm Brawner, & A. Stinchcomb be appointed Commissioner from Elbert Court house, to Dudley ferry, Saml Woods, Robt Moon, Saml Patton, from Dudleys to the furnace, from Stokeses, Saml Nelson, John McCurdy, Allen Leper, be and the same is hereby appointed Commissioners to report to next Inferior Court, agreeable to the recommendation of the Grand Jury.

On Application, it is Ordered, that William Barnett be and he is hereby appointed Guardian for Jonathan Sutton, Charles Goss for Nelly Sutton, Benjamin Brown for Colley Sutton, and Isaac Suttle for Salley, Joel, & George Sutton, on their Complying with the Law in such Cases made and provided.

Ordered, that Charles Bedningfield, Junr be and he is hereby appointed Overseer on the broad River Roaad that leads from Odems ferry to Elbert Court house, from Deep Creek to fergues Creek, George Stoovall, and from the Cross Road before mentioned to Cedr Creek, Jessey Whight, from Ceder Creek to the fish dam ford, Samuel Clark, and from thence to Warhatchee creek, Lewis Mosley, from thence to Coodies Creek, M. J. Williams, and from Coodes Creek to Petersburgh and also from Stephens ford on Broad River into said Road, Thomas Coleman.

From Elberton to James Huffs, Edmond Lowry, from said Huffs to the fish dam foard, Joel Crafford

From the Franklin line to Dixons, Daniel Parker, from Dixons to Furgues Creek, Edward [102]
Story.

Barnabas Pace, from the Franklin line (on the ~~broad~~ Road leading from franklin Court house to Elberton) to the furnace Road Crossing at ~~bowers~~ Browns Mill, and Robert Brown, from said Road to Olivers Store.

Luke White, from the County line on the Road passing Robt Pulliams to Elberton, to the hollow Spring, John Nelms, from said spring to Olivers Store.

Thomas Oliver, from his store to Larken Gatewood, Larken Gatewood from thence to Elberton.

Francis Cook, from the Court house, to the Cross Road at or near his own plantation, William Hightowr, from said Cross Road to the Uper End of John P. Harper plantation, Thomas Wooldridge, from thence to the fork of the Road near to William Thompsons, Saml McGehee, from Allens Mill on Beaverdam Creek to the fork of the Road near William Taits, William Tait, from Alstons ford on Beaverdam Creek to Elisha Towns, Job Hammond, From thence to Thomas Taits, Thomas Tait, from thence to the Junction with Broad River Road.

Thomas S. Carter, from the Bever Dam near Co^{lo} Higginbotham to Elberton.

Robert Moon, from Lightwood Logg Creek to bigg Cedar Creek, from thence to the forks of the Road above Co^{lo} Cun

---

Cunninghams, Angush Johnson, and from the fork of said Road to Vanns Creek meeting house, Benj^{h} Head, from thence to Allens Mill on Beaverdam, Henry Gaines.

Joel Doss, from the fork of the Road above Cunninghams to Alexandria Warehouse, John Moore, from said warehouse opposite Richard Colbert, James Alston from thence to Alstons ford on Beaverdam.

James McDonald, from Shockleys ferry to Thomas Hookers, from thence to Samuel Shield, Esqr, Robert Black, James Hart to the Holley springs, Larken Curry, from Hugh McDonald to James Jones Little Cold Water, from thence to Joshua Underwoods, James Riley, and Richard Bond, from said Underwoods to Co^{lo} Higginbotham, Thomas Kees, from Allens Mill B. dam to Cherokee ford.

Jonathan Phair }
vs } Award
Angus Johnson }
et al }

We, Moses Haynes, Elijah [faint], Thomas Woodward, John B. Alexander, Patrick Mitchel, Julyan Nail, Junr, and James Highsmith, being Chosen as Arbitrators, in a suit of damages of assault & battery, Jonathan Phair vs Angus Johnson, Archeble Johnson, John McDonald, Junr, and John McDonald, Senr, James Brown, Junr, Daniel Johnson, Malcum Johnson, W^{m} McKinzey, and Angus McDonald, after taking the Evidence in the above suit, and Duly examined the same, do adjudge & award that Jonathan

Jonathan Phair, the plaintiff, do draw the suit and pay all Lawfull cost. Given under our hand and seales, this 15th day of July 1799. [103]

Patrick Mitchell
J. Neal
James Highsmith

M. Hayens
E. Owens
Thos Woodward
John B. Alexander

The following Persons was drawn to serve on the Petit Jury at the Next term, to wit.

N^{o}

1. Robt Burton
2. Reuben Jones
3. David Hudson
4. Wm Felps
5. Booker Easter
6. Burrly Greenwood
7. Ch^{s} Bedningfield
8. Henry Jackson
9. Thos Doogles
10. Brown Dye
11. Arthur Jones
12. Joseph Downer
13. Wm Runnold
14. Jer^{h} Sutton
15. Jere^{h} Walker
16. John Waller
17. David Neel
18. Silvanus Stokes
19. Drury Town
20. Thos King
21. Joshua Andwool
22. Jesse Rowell
23. Jesse Vincent
24. Nelson Johnson
25. James Riley
26. David Adams
27. Eliab Vincent
28. Minor Marsh
29. Joseph Bond
30. Wm Thompson
31. And^{w} Cunningham
32. John Parnal
33. Sherod Morris
34. Stephen Groves
35. Benjn Nail
36. Math^{s} Ward
37. Elisha Town
38. Wm Appleby
39. Robt Black
40. Alex^{r} Thompson
41. Wm Cockthron
42. John McDonald
43. Nathl Etcherson
44. Wm Hodge

---

45. Jonathan Vineyard
46. Moses Hunt
47. James Highmith
48. David Brown
49. Thos Howell
50. Harvey Allen
51. Gabriel Smith

At an Inferior Court held at Elberton, the 10th day of February 1800.

Present, Wm Barnett, R. Hunt, R. Banks, Saml Higginbotham, R. Allen, Esqrs

Sarah Walker }
Henry G. Walker & }
James M. Carter }
vs }
Thomas Carter }

Jury Sworn, to wit.

1. William Felps	7. James Riley
2. Beverly Greenwood	8. Elisha Towns
3. Arthur Jones	9. Gabriel Smith
4. Joseph Downer	10. Henry Jackson
5. Silvanus Stokes	11. Thomas Napir
6. Thomas King	12. Asa Thompson

We the Jury find for the plaintiff One Hundred and thirty Eight Dollars and Forty Cents.

Thomas Napier

Joseph Cook & } [104]
Elizabeth W. Cook }
Admrx of J. Thompson, Decd }
vs } Case
Tryon Harris & }
C. Harris }

I do hereby Confess Judgment for the sum of one hundred and Eighty six Dollars and fifty Cents, With Interest from 2nd day August 1796.

Tryon Harris

Manus Lumby }
vs }
James Crow }

Jury Sworn, to wit.

1. David Hudson	7. Drury Towns
2. Maths Ward	8. John Blake

3. Robert Black	9. Benjamin Brown
4. James Highsmith	10. Wm Criddenton
5. Wm Robins	11. Henry Mosley
6. Nathan James	12. James Oliver

We Find for the plaintiff Forty three dollars, twelve and a half Cents, with Interest and Cost.

David Hudson, for^{n}

George & E. Cook }
adm^{rs} J. Thompson, Dec^{d} }
vs }
Tryon Harris & D. Harris }

Dism^{d} at Def^{t} Cost.

George Cook & }
E. Cook }
vs }
C. Harris & Darven Harris }

Dismised Def^{t} Cost.

—

Wm Aycock }
vs }
Robert Moore }

The Same Jury as in The Case Carter vs Carter.

We the Jury find for the plaintiff twenty three Dollars and thirty Cents, with Cost.

Thomas Napier

The Court then adjourned till To Morrow ten o'Clock.

R. Hunt, R. Banks, R. Allen, S. Higginbotham

Tuesday 11th

The Court met Pursuant to Adjournment.

John R. Ragland }
vs }
Henry G. Walker }

Jury Sworn, to wit.

1. Wm Felps	7. Joseph Downer
2. Thomas King	8. Elisha Towns
3. Henry Jackson	9. Asa Thompson
4. Beverly Greenwood	10. Silvanus Stokes
5. James Riley	11. Gabriel Smith
6. Thos Napier	12. Elisha Brown

We the Jury find for the plaintiff Three dollars.

Thos Napier

~~Wm Aycock~~ } [105]
vs }
~~Robert Moore~~ }

~~The Same Jury as in the Case Carter vs Carter.~~

~~We the Jury find for the Plaintiff.~~

Benjamin Cook }
vs }
Gerald Walthal }

Jury Sworn (to wit)

1. Wm Arnold	7. Arthur Jones
2. Edwd Clark	8. David Hudson
3. Maths Ward	9. M. Farman
4. Wm Oliver	10. Ben Brown
5. David Everhart	11. Job Hammond
6. James H. Smith	12. W. Haynes

We the Jury find for the defendant.

Wm Oliver

John Teasley }
vs }
Gab[l] Higginbotham }

William Criddenton, the Common Bail, Came In to Court and Surrendered his principal. Ordered, that the defendant remain in Custody Untill he gives Sec[y], When Gabriel Higginbotham, the Defendant, & Caleb Higginbotham, the Security, came Into Court And Acknowledged them Selves Indebted to the plaintiff in double the Sum mentioned in the Sheriff Bail Bounds, Conditioned that if the Said Gabriel Should be cast in the above suit, that he the

---

Defendant will pay the Condemnation money, or surrender himself As the law Directs &c, or I will do it for him. Witness our hands, the 17th day of Feb[y]1800.

Attest. M. Woods

G. Higginbotham
Caleb Higginbotham

R. Hunt, R. Banks, R. Allen, S. Higginbotham

The Court then adjourned Untill tomorrow ten o'Clock.

Wednesday, the 18th

The Court met pursuant to adjournment.

Gerald Walthall }
vs } Slander
Benjamin Cook }

Jury Sworn, to wit.

1. W[m] Felps
2. Tho[s] King
3. David Eberhart
4. B. Greenwood
5. James Riley
6. Evan Ragland
7. Jo[s] Downer
8. D. Hudson
9. Tho[s] Napier
10. Sylvanus Stokes
11. Arther Jones
12. Ben Brown

We the Jury find for the plaintiff Two Hundred & Seventy five dollars.

Tho[s] Napier

On the Petition of John Staples, Esq[r]. [106]

Ordered, that Forrester Upshaw be appointed a Constable for said Staples District, he Complying With the Law in Such Case made and provided.

Gideon Davis }
vs } Case
Thos Woodridge }

Thos Woodridge }
in right of his wife }
vs } Case
Absolom Davis }
And Others }

In the above Cases, by Consent of parties, it is agreed that They Shall be removed to the Superior Court and there to Submited to Special Jury, it is also further agreed by the parties, that Gideon Davis was one of the youngest children of Ann Davis, being at the Time of death of Wm Hackney, Under whose will the parties Claim the property, the Subject of the above Suits, and that Hezekiah Wooldridge, the wife of Thomas Wooldridge, was one of the youngest Children living at the Time of the death of Mrs Ann Davis, who was the daughter

---

Of Wm Hackney, who in the said will had a life estate in a Certain Negroe wench Called Juno, and her increase, that there are in Existence thereby five Negroes, descendants of the said wench Juno, and that the Negroes Specified and Mentioned in the declarations of the above Suits, one part of that number Thomas Wooldridge holds in his possession, those claimed at the Suit of Gideon Davis, and that those Claimed at the Suit of Thomas Wooldridge are in possession of Absalom Davis, Senr, Gideon Davis, & Joseph Davis (Viz) in the possession of Gideon Davis, two fellows Will & Cesar, In the possession of Joseph Davis, two fellows Jack & Jim, the Balance in the possession of Absalom Davis, Senr, that the above Cases Shall be Submitted to the Jury on the Construction of the will, the facts as above Stated being hereby agreed To by the parties, all exceptions to the writs waved.

Mathews, Att^y for Wooldridge
John Griffin for Davis

Samuel Hunter } [107]
vs }
John King }

Jury Sworn (to wit)

1. Samuel Clarke
2. James Hannah
3. Mish Lowery
4. Thomas Smith
5. Peter Johnson
6. Johthⁿ Phair
7. Francis Phair
8. Wᵐ Whaley
9. Jacob Odem
10. Geo. Gerald
11. Wᵐ Blankingship
12. A. Stinchcomb

We the Jury find for the Plaintiff Thirty Six Dollars.

Jacob Odem, forⁿ

Joshua Roberts }
vs }
Evan Ragland }

Jury Sworn, to wit.

1. Wᵐ Phelps
2. Burley Greenwood
3. Joseph Downer
4. Sylvanus Stokes
5. Thomas King
6. James Riley
7. David Hudson
8. Arthur Jones
9. David Everhart
10. Richᵈ Bonds
11. Thomas Napier
12. Benjamin Brown

We the Jury find for the plaintiff one hundred and Eighty Six Dollars.

Thomas Napier

James Thurman }
vs }
John H. Johnson }

The Same Jury as in the Case Roberts vs Ragland.

We the Jury find for the plaintiff Fifty Dollars, with Cost.

Thoˢ Napier

Thomas Chiders }
vs }
John Colbert }
James Dudley }

The Same Jury as in the above Case.

We the Jury find for the plaintiff Two Hundred & three Dollars.

Thomas Napier

William Dudley Came Into Court and Acknowledged himself Security in terms of the Law.

Test. M. Woods — W^{m} X Dudley his mark

Leroy Pope }
vs } Case
Abraham Colson }

I hereby Confess Judg^{t} on Hundred & Fifty one dollars and Eighty Seven Cents.

A. Colson

Leroy Pope }
vs }
Abraham Colson }

I hereby Confess Judgement For the Sum of one hundred and Seventy five Dollars & Eighty four Cents.

Test. P. Early — A. Colston

The Court then adjourned till Tomorrow ten o'Clock. [108]

R. Hunt, R. Banks, R. Allen, S. Higginbotham

Thursday, 13th

Court met Pursuant to adjournment.

Present, William Barnett, R. Hunt, Reuben Allen, Esqr

Moses Terrell }
vs }
James Kidd }

Jury Sworn, to wit.

1. Wm Felps
2. Thos King
7. Joseph Downer
8. Arther Jones

3. Ri[d] Bond	9. Benjamin Brown
4. Bev Greenwood	10. Sylvanus Stokes
5. James Riley	11. D. Aberhart
6. Thomas Napier	12. Lenard Turman

We the Jury find for the plaintiff One Hundred and fourteen Dollars And Seventy Five Cents.

Tho[s] Napier

Sally S. Bibb }
vs } att
Ben Andrew }

Judgment by Default.

John Spier }
vs } Case
Samuel Goolsby & }
John Dorsey }

The Same Jury as in the Case Terrell vs Kidd.

We the Jury find for the plaintiff Sixty Two Dollars Fifty Cents, with Interest from the 12th October 1797, & Cost.

Tho[s] Napier

Mary Phair }
vs }
Jonathan Phair }

The Same Jury as in the Above.

We the Jury find for the plaintiff Three Hundred and thirty four Dollars and fifty cents, within Interest on the Notes.

Tho[s] Napier

Solomon Roundall }
vs }
Lewis B. Thompson }

Jury Sworn, to wit.

1. David Hudson	7. John Winkfield
2. H. G. Walker	8. Wyatt Right
3. Henry Lyon	9. Fran. Phair
4. Moses Haynes	10. Wm Brown
5. G. Turman	11. Jacob Odem
6. Nathl Smith	12. Ben Fortson

We the Jury find for the plaintiff Twenty Nine dollars Eighty five & ¾ Cents.

H. G. Walker

Wm H. Tait }
vs }
Eli Eavenson } [109]

The Same Jury as in the Case Terrell vs Kidd.

We the Jury find for the plaintiff forty Dollars.

Thomas Napier

William Dudley }
vs } Trespass
Samuel Post }

Under the penalty of five Hundred Dollars, We agree to Submit the above Cause to the final Determination and Arbitration of John Staples, Saml Nelson, & Samuel Woods, their award To be made & returned to the Next Inferior Court for Elbert County.

A. Martin, Plff Attorney
C. Tait

Ezekiel King }
vs }
W. Blankenship }

The Same Jury as in the Case Terrell vs Kidd.

We the Jury find the plaintiff Eighty Seven Dollars and forty Nine Cents.

Thos Napier

—

R. Thompson }
vs }
George Blackwell }

The Same Jury as in the last Case.

We the Jury find for the Plaintiff forty eight dollars.

Tho[s] Napier

Roger Atkerson }
vs } Deb[t]
George Darden }

Jury Sworn, to wit.

1. David Hudson	7. Jn[o] Wingfield
2. H. G. Walker	8. Wyatt Right
3. Henry Lyon	9. Francis Phair
4. M. Haynes	10. W[m] Brown
5. G. Turman	11. Jacob Odem
6. Nath[l] Smith	12. Ben Fortson

We the Jury find for the plaintiff One Hundred and Eighty Dollars and Sixty four and one quarter Cents.

& 62½/100 H. G. Walker, for[n]

Pope & Walker }
vs } Case
W[m] Sharp }

I Confess Judgement for forty four Dollars and Sixty four [smear] one quarter Cents.

W[m] Sharp

James Freeman } [110]
vs }
Jonathan Arnold }
& Moses Haynes }

The Same Jury as in the case King vs Blankingship.

We the Jury find for the plaintiff ninty seven dollars, with Interest from the date.

Thomas Napier

James Freeman }
vs } Case
Moses Haynes }

the Same Jury as in the above case.

We the Jury find for the plaintiff Two hundred and Eleven dollars with Interest.

Tho[s] Napier

Solomon Rountree }
vs }
Francis Powell }

The Same Jury as above.

We the Jury find for the plaintiff ninty three Dollars, with Interest.

Thomas Napier

Zimry Tait }
vs } Debt
John Appling }
Ch[s] Williamson }
M. Woods }

The Same Jury as in the last case.

We the Jury find for the plaintiff Three hundred and Eighty three dollars, with Interest.

Tho. Napier

James Kidd }
& James Floyd }
vs }
Jn[o] Greenwood }

James Kidd }
vs }
John Greenwood }

We, the under written Arbitrators, having, on this twenty Eighth day of December 1798, at the house of James Kidd, arbitrate all matters in dispute between James Kidd and John Greenwood, have duly considered all matters brought before us, and defend in behalf of James Kidd on a bond from said Greenwood, the Sum of Two Hundred and Sixty five dollars, with Cost of Suit, likewise on a Note for one Thousand weight of Tobacco, a balance in favour of Said Kidd Ninteen dollars and Ninty three Cents, with cost of suit. Given under our hands the day and date above Ritten.

R. Allen, Joseph Rucker
Th^{o} Fortson, John Rucker
William Allen

Court then adjourned till Nine o'Clock Tomorrow.

R. Hunt, R. Banks, R. Allen, Esq^{rs}

Friday, 14th

Court met Pursuant to adjournment.

Present, Wm Barnett, R. Hunt, R. Allen, Esq^{rs}

Woods & Lindsay } [111]
vs }
Gabriel Higginbotham }

Jury Sworn, to wit.

1. Wm Felps	7. D. Eberhart
2. L. Turman	8. H. Criddenton
3. N. Smith	9. Joseph Downer
4. Arthur Jones	10. Benjamin Brown
5. Wm Brown	11. G. Greenwood
6. Stephen Smith	12. Beverly Greenwood

We the Jury find for the plaintiff Two hundred and Twenty Two dollars and seventy four Cents & Interest.

Wm Brown, fore^{n}

Beverly Greenwood }
vs }
John Greenwood }
& George Greenwood }

Jury Sworn (to wit)

1. Wm Feleps	7. Henry Criddenton
2. A. Jones	8. N. Smith
3. E. Hart	9. Stephen Smith
4. Benjn Brown	10. Joseph Downer
5. L. Turman	11. Jacob Odem
6. Wm Brown	12. Thos Y. Gill

We the Jury find for the plaintiff one hundred And Sixteen Dollars and fifty Cents, with Interest.

Wm Brown, for^n^

Caty Bradberry }
by her Guardian }
vs } Slander
Preston Miller }

The Same Jury as in the above Case, Except Jacob Odem, Arther Skinner.

thereof

We the Jury find for the plaintiff five Hundred and Eight Dollars.

Wm Brown

—

Robert Thompson }
vs } Case
Robert Singleton }

Settled, Defendants Cost.

Wm Moore }
vs } Attachment
Wm Daniel }

The Same Jury as in the last Case.

We the Jury find for the plaintiff One hundred And Eighty eight dollars fifty Cents, with Interest from the 27th of April 1799.

Wm Brown

It appearing that Garrett Turman was Summoned as a Garnashee in the above case, & he having deposed that he had in his hands fifty Nine dollars and Fifty Cents due to the said Daniel at the time of Levying of said attachment. It is ordered by the court, that Judgement be entered up against the said Turman infavor of said Moore for that amount.

Rountree & Taylor }
vs } att^{t}
Clem Turman }

the Same Jury as in the Above Case.

We the Jury find for the plaintiff three Hundred Seventeen dollars and fifty Seven Cents, with Interest.

Wm Brown

John Moore }
vs }
John Greenwood }

Settled, Defendants Cost.

Solomon Rountree } [112]
vs }
John Howthon }

I confess Judgment for Sixty Dollars, with Interest from the Twenty fifth day of December 1798.

John Hauthon

Edward Walthal acknowledged himself Sec^{y} in terms of the Law.

Edward Walthal

John Carrell }
vs }
Ephraim Allen }

Settled, defendant Cost.

Drury Thompson }
vs } Case
Tarter Thompson }
& L. B. Thompson }

Discontinued.

Anamas Cooper & C° }
vs } Case
Sally S. Bibb E[x] }
W[m] Bibb, Dec[d] }

Settled, at mutual Cost.

R. Hunt, R. Banks, R. Allen

The Court then adjourned till Tomorrow ten o'Clock.

Saturday, 15th

Court met pursuant to adjournment.

Present, R. Hunt, R. Allen, S. Higginbotham, R. Banks, Esq[rs]

Ordered, that John Morris and over River Jourdon Be appointed Constables for Cap[t] Alexanders district, the Complying with the law in Such Cases made and provided.

On petition of Samuel McGhee, Thomas Oliver, & Woods & C°, praying that they might obtain Licence to Keep a Tavern at their Respective houses.

Ordered, that the same be Granted, on their Complying with the requists of the Law in Such Cases.

John Nelms Came into Court and Surrendered up David Nelms and George Blackwell. Ordered, that they remain in Custody.

Reuben Eastin Came into Court & Surrened up John Greenwood. Ordered, that he remain in Custody of the Sheriff.

On Motion of Rowland Brown, Stating to the Court, that David Nelms was Confined in Gail, for whom he Stood bound for his appearance to the present term. Ordered, that he be detained Untill he gives Special bail, or other wise discharged by Law.

Richard George } [113]
vs }
River Jourdon }

Settled, mutual Cost.

George Evans }
vs } Case
John Booth }

I Confess Judgement for One Hundred dollars, on account of a stay of Execution for twelve Months.

John Booth
Feby 16th 1800

The Court then adjourned till Court in Course.

R. Hunt, R. Banks, R. Allen, S. Higginbotham

May 5th 1800

Present, Samuel Higginbotham, Esqr.

The Following persons was drawn to Serve as Jurors at the next term, Viz.

N°
1. Henry Burton
2. William Johnson
3. Francis Ellis
4. Thomas Lovelady
5. Wm Bennett
6. Charles Smith
7. Samuel Self
8. Wm Settles
9. Isaac Morris
10. Martin Deadwiler
11. Joseph Morris
12. Francis Gilley
13. Thomas Dooley
14. Robert Smith
15. Wm Graham
16. David Morgan
17. Wm Guttery
18. John Decker
19. Preston Miller
20. Joel Miller
21. Wm Davis
22. Edward Lyon
23. Wm Fortson
24. Thomas Hooker
25. George Turman
26. James Mann

---

27. Henry Gains
28. Joseph Huddleston
29. John Owen
30. Joseph Allen
31. Thomas Cameron
32. Daniel Brockington
33. James Burden
40. Thomas Camron
41. Nathl Williford
42. Wm Fergus
43. Wm Vickory
44. Thomas Connelly
45. Absalom Trantham
46. Jno Forbus

34. Wm Guttery
35. McCarty Oliver
36. David Montgomery
37. Thomas Haney
38. Isham Goss
39. John Smith
47. Edward Denney
48. Partrick Peace
49. Hugh Harcrow
50. Francis Baty
51. Wm Sorrels
52. Robert Pulliam

At an Inferior Court begun and held at Elberton, the 14th day of July 1800.

Present, Wm Barnett, R. Allen, Ralph Banks, Saml Higginbotham, R. Hunt, Esq^{rs}

E~~dward~~manuel Wombusee }
vs }
Hugh McDonald }

Jury Sworn, to wit.

1. Edward Lyon
2. McCarty Oliver
3. Arther Jones
4. George Turman
5. Fra^{s} Batey
6. Henry Gains
7. Joseph Huddleston
8. Burgutt Green
9. Benjn Brown
10. John Owen
11. Wm Cross
12. Thos Napier

We the Jury find for the plaintiff Two hundred and forty two Dollars & forty eight Cents.

Thos Napier

Benjamin Brown } [114]
vs }
Joseph Huddleston }

Jury Sworn, To wit.

1. Wm Fortson
2. Wm Grimes
3. John Decker
4. Wm Oliver
5. Thomas Smith
6. James Childres
7. Wm Carter
8. Edmund Shackleford
9. Christopher Harris
10. M. Fannen
11. H. Collins
12. W. Blankinship

We the Jury find for the plaintiff the Sum of one hundred and fifteen dollars and thirty cents, with cost of Suit.

Wm Oliver, for^n^

Woods & Lindsay }
vs }
Abner Pulor }

Nath[l] Alston, The Bail below, came into Court and Surrendered his principal, where upon he was discharged.

When Abner Pulor, the defendant, and John Pollard, Security, came unto court and acknowledged Themselves Indebted to the plaintiffs in double the Sum Mentioned in the Sheriff Bail Bond, Conditioned that if the Said Abner Pulor be cast in the above Suit, that he the defendant will pay the Condemnation Money, or Surrender himself as the Law directs, or I will do it for him. Witness our hands, the 14th day of July 1800.

Abner Pulor, John Pollard

George & Elizabeth Cook }
Adm[r] of the Estate }
Isham Thompson }
vs }
James Kidd }

Jury N[o] 1.

We the Jury find for the plaintiff fifty three dollars & twenty three Cents.

Thomas Napier

John Hutt }
vs }
W[m] Winn }

Nonsuit.

James Kidd }
vs } Att[t]
Reuben Frazier }

Dismised.

John Kenedy }
vs } Case
Thomas Lovelady }

Settled.

John McKee }
vs } Debt
Hugh McDonald }

Settled, at defendants Cost.

Woods & Lindsay }
vs }
David Nelms }

Jury Sworn, to wit.

1. Wm Fortson	7. Wm Carter
2. Wm Graham	8. C. Harris
3. John Duke	9. Henry Collins
4. Wm Oliver	10. Henry Mosley
5. Thomas Smith	11. James Shackleford
6. James Childres	12. W. Blankinship

We the Jury find for the plaintiff the Sum of one hundred & two Dollars, thirty Seven ¾ Cents, being the principle and Interest of both note & Due bill, also the defendant to pay Cost.

Wm Oliver, fore^n^

Thompson & Watkins }
vs } Case
John & Spencer Algood }

The same Jury as in the case Geo. & E. Cook vs J. Kidd.

We the Jury find for the plaintiffs forty Dollars & Eighty Cents.

Thomas Napier

James Blair } [115]
vs }
Benjn Head }

The Jury as in the above Case.

We the Jury find for the plaintiff forty four Dollars and forty Six Cents.

James Shackleford came in and } Th° Napier
acknowledged himself bound ac^{g} to Law. }

John Wingfield }
vs }
Gabriel Higginbotham }
& John Sweezie }

The Same Jury as in the Case Woods & Lindsay vs David Nelms.

We the Jury find for the plaintiff the Sum of fifty Dollars, Seventy Seven Cents, being the principal and Interest due together, with Cost Suit.

Wm Oliver, fore^{n}

Benjamin Brown }
vs }
Joseph Huddleston }

July Term 1800 Inferior Court at the term aforesaid.

The parties came into Court, when the above case was called on for Trial. Council for the defendant Excepted to the evidence of the plaintiff, upon the following grounds. The action was founded on a note of hand for the payment of Tobacco. The note was dated 21st Sep^{t} 1797, made payable on the 25th of Decr next, insuing the date of the note. the exception the Court over ruled, all the Exceptions to the writ had been previously waved & one Term formerly given.

P. Allen, Def^{t} Atty

The Court adjourned untill tomorrow morning Ten O'clock.

July 15th 1800

The Court met pursuant to adjournment.

Present, Wm Barnett, R. Hunt, Saml Higginbotham, R^{n} Allen, Esquires

C. Harris, for the use }
of Young, Miller & C° }
vs }
Jn° R. Ragland }

Jury Sworn, viz.

1. Edward Lyon
2. McCarty Oliver
3. John Owen
4. H. Gaines
5. Jo^{s} Huddleston
6. Arthur Jones
7. Jn° Montgomery
8. Saml Shields
9. B. Brown
10. Wm Cook
11. J. Shackleford
12. B. Green

We find for the Defendant.

Saml Shields, foreman

In the above case, the plaintiffs pray an Appeal, which is Granted.

Reuben Satewhite }
vs }
Jn° Middleton }

Judgement confessed for the Sum of 85 Dollars & 32 Cents & Cost & Stay of Execution three months.

Jn° Teasley }
vs }
Gabriel Higginbotham }

Same Jury as before.

In this Case, a Jurer is ordered to be withdrawn & the case continued.

Geo. Tillman & } [116]
Jeremiah Stacks }
vs }
W^{m} McCune }

I confess Judgement for the Sum of Eighty Dollars & Six Cents, & Interest from the date of the note, with Stay of Levy three months.

Walton, for Def^{t}

Wm Chislom }
vs }
John F. Garrell }
C. Sales }

The defendant, John F. Garrell, now at this time, Comes into Court and Confess Judgement for the Sum of forty three dollars, Sixty two Cents, with Lawfull Interest & Cost.

John F. Gerald

Wm Chislom }
vs }
John F. Gerald }

July Term 1800

Now, at this term, the defendant Confesses Judg^t for the Sum of fifty three dollars, with Lawfull Interest & Cost.

John F. Gerrald

John Andrew }
vs }
Thomas Y. Gill }

The Same Jury as in the case Miller & Co vs Jno R. Ragland.

We the Jury find for the plaintiff seventy Eight dollars.

Saml Shields, foreman

Geo. & E. Cook }
Adm^r of Isham Thompson }
vs }
Evan Ragland & }
Wm Hatcher }

The defendant came unto Court and Confessed Judg^t to the Plaintiff for the Sum of three Hundred and ten dollars, with Interest from the Second of August on Thousand Seven hundred and ninty Six, with Cost of Suit, with Six months Stay of Execution.

J. C. Walton

Tho[s] Hudson }
vs } Case
G. Higginbotham }

The Same Jury as in the cas Andrew vs Gill.

We the Jury find for the plaintiff fifty four dollars & Sixty Six cents.

Sam[l] Shields, Foreman

Joseph Neal }
vs } Case
John McMullen }

The Same Jury.

We the Jury we find for the Plaintiff Two hundred and Seventy Seven dollars and Sixty eight Cents.

Sam[l] Shields, For.

Josiah Sartain }
vs }
Robins Andrew }
& W[m] H. Moon }

The defendant came into Court and confessed Judg[t] to the plaintiff for the Sum of one hundred & fifty dollars, with Interest from the 25th day of December 1799, with cost of Suit, with a Stay of Execution Six months. 15th July 1800

C. Tait, Atty for Deft.

Robert L. Tait } [117]
vs } Case
Robert Martin }

The Same Jury as in the case Andrew vs Gill.

We the Jury find for the plaintiff forty nine dollars.

Sam[l] Shields, for.

John Banks }
vs } Case
M. Haynes & Co }

I confess Judgement for the Sum of one hundred and ninty one dollars and Seventy five Cents, with Interest from the first day of October 1799, with Stay three months.

C. Tait, Atty for Deft.

John Williamson }
vs } Case
Wm Brown & }
Jesse Hendrick }

The Same Jury as in the case Andrew vs Gill.

We the Jury find for the plaintiff one hundred & four dollars.

Saml Shields, for^{n}

~~Samelly~~ Sally L. Bibb }
vs }
John Andrew, Grdn }

The Same Jury as in the Andrew vs Gill.

We the Jury find for the defendant.

Saml Shields, for^{n}

—

Memorable Walker }
vs } Attach^{t}
Wm Akin }

Daniel L. Waller being Summoned as Garnashee in the above case, and having deposed that he hath in his hands thirty two dollars and one half of the property of Wm Akin. on Motion of C. Tait, atty for the plaintiff, it is ordered that Judgement be entered up against the Said Daniel for the Said Amount.

Memorable Walker }
vs } Att^{t}
Wm Akin }

The Same Jury as in the case Andrew vs Gill.

We the Jury find for the plaintiff ninety five Dollars & forty Cents.

Sam[l] Shields

The Court then adjourned untill tomorrow ten O'Clock.

Wednesday, 16th

The Court met pursuant to adjournment.

Present, W[m] Barnett, R. Hunt, Ralph Banks, R. Allen, S. Higginbotham, Esqr[s]

On the petition of Laughlin Currey, Hugh McDonald, Leonard Keeling, Jeremiah Walker, & John Ragland praying that the might obtain a Licence to Keep a tavern at their respective Dwelling houses.

Ordered, that the Same be Granted, on their complying with the requisits of the Law in Such Cases.

The Court proceeded to appoint Inspectors for the present year for the diferent ware houses in Elbert County, when Thomas Burton, Joel Crawford, & R. Easter was appointed for Olivers Ware house, Charles Taylor, Francis Satewhite, Jun[r], & William Watkins for Watkins Ware house, and henry Harper, W[m] Alexander, & John Cason for the ware house at the mouth of Cold Water, and James Wood, Jn[o] Wilhite, & Robert Moon for Wilhites Ware house, and Edmond Shackleford, John Blake, & Reuben Easton for Eastons Ware House.

The Court then adjourned till tomorrow nine O'clock.

Thursday, 17th the Court met pursuant to adjournment.

Present, W[m] Barnett, R. Hunt, R. Allen, S. Higginbotham

On the petition of James Kidd.

Ordered, that he Obtain a Licence to Keep a tavern at his dwelling house in Elberton, on his Complying with requisites of the Law in Such Cases.

Susannah Collins }
vs }
Henry Collins }

Settled.

Thomas Waters }
vs } Case
Jesse Colbert & }
Wm Colbert }

Settled.

Present, Samuel Higginbotham, Esquire [119]

Jurors Drawn for this Term (To Wit)

1. John Moore
2. Henry Muckle
3. James Dudley
4. Thomas Hay
5. James Arnold
6. Utterbridge Dixon
7. Frederick McGuire
8. John McMurtery
9. John Beck
10. Benjn Cook, Junr
11. James Morris
12. James Turman
13. John Hamm
14. Thos Burges
15. William Cross
16. William Carter
17. James Lawson
18. Saml Carr
19. John Algood
20. Arthur Forbus
21. Joseph Pulliam
22. Warren Moore
23. Josiah Sartin
24. Willes Rucker
25. Stephen Mobley
26. Robert Wood
27. Joseph Calvert
28. Joshua Fields
29. Francis Phair
30. Clabourn
31. Toren Merrit
32. Joseph Albert
33. Burket Green
34. John Maye
35. John Millican
36. Ephraim Moss
37. Frederick Heart
38. Edmond Lowry
39. James Jones
40. Robert Moons
41. Quinton Shannon
42. Drury Thompson, Junr
43. Fedrick Davis
44. Absalom Little
45. Archer Burden
46. John Maxwell
47. John Nelms
48. Spencer Algood
49. John Jones
50. Josiah Dobb
51. Aron Johnson
52. John McKee
53. Thomas Brady

54. James Childres

At an Inferior Court held at Elbert Court house.

The 9th day of February 1801

Present, Wm Barnett, R. Hunt, R. Allen, R. Banks, Sm^{l} Higginbotham, Esqr^{s}

George Greenwood }
vs } Case
John Greenwood }

Jury Sworn (to wit)

1. James Arnold	7. Burket Green
2. Thomas Burges	8. Spencer Algood
3. Wm Cross	9. James Childres
4. Wm Carter	10. Jno White
5. John Algood	11. Saml Clark
6. Joseph Pulliam	12. Benjamin Brown

We the Jurors find for the plaintiff on Hundred & Seventeen Dollars and fifty Cents, with Costs.

Joseph Pulliam

Daven Harris }
vs } Case
Wm Thompson}

The Same Jury as in the above case.

We the Jurors find for the plaintiff Seventy Dollars, with Cost.

Joseph Pulliam, F. M.

Woods & Lindsay }
vs } Debt
Abner Peelor }

With Drawn.

Wm Cross }
vs }
John Gober } [120]

Withdrawn.

James Heard }
vs } Dueit
George Rucker, Senr }
George Rucker }

Withdrawn.

Wm Dudley }
vs } Trespass
Saml Post }

Refered and award returned In The words following.

We, Henry Gatewood & Levin Wailes, arbitrators, in a Matter depending Between Wm Dudley and Samuel Post, after having Heard all the evidence, relative to the Several matters in Controversy between the Said parties, and deliberating maturely on the business, do give it as our Opinions, that each of the parties Shall pay their own cost in the Suit depending in the Inferior Court of Elbert County, and Instituted by the Said Dudley against the Said Post, and that the payment of Such Costs Shall Exonerate each of the Said parties from any damages for or on account of any Trespasses Supposed, Trespass Commited on the other at any time previous to this date & in this opinion, I James

---

James Woods being Called upon as a thirds Man do concur. Witness our hands, this Seventh day of January 1801.

Henry Gatewood, Levin Wailes, James Wood

The Court then adjourned till 9 o'clock To morrow.

Tuesday 10th

The Court met pursuant to Adjournment.

Woods & Lindsay }
vs }
John Fain }

Charles Fain and Thomas Phelps, the Bail below, Came Into Court, and Surrendered his principal and they were discharged, when Charles Fain acknowledged himself bound as the Law directs.

Woods & Lindsay }
vs }
Wm Cross }

Withdrawn.

John Teasley }
vs }
Gab^l Higginbotham }

Jury Sworn, to Witt.

1. Saml Carr
2. Toren Merrit
3. John Millicam
4. Abs^m Little
5. John Nelms

6. Robert Burks
7. David Robertson
8. Lewis Moseley
9.Joshua Tyner [121]
10. John Rowsey
11. John Murrah
12. John Smith

We the Jury find for the plaintiff the Sum of one Hundred and Eighty Dollars, with Interest and Cost of Suit.

Joshua Tyner, fore Man

Thomas Glascock for }
the use E. Ragland }
vs }
vs }
Jno Cunningham }

the Jury as in the above case.

We the Jury find for the plaintiff $144.42 Cents, with Interest & Cost.

Joshua Tyner, for^n

Woods & Lindsay }
vs }
Rob[t] Kennedy }

Jury Sworn, to wit.

1. Sam[l] Karr	7. L. Mosley
2. Torren Merrit	8. Joshua Tyner
3. A. Little	9. John Rowsey
4. John Nelms	10. John Murrah
5. Robert Burks	11. John Smith
6. David Robertson	12. Z. Clark

we find for the plaintiff the Sum of Two Hundred & Ninety Seven Dollars & Eighty four cents, with Interest & Cost.

Joshua Tyner

Garland Wingfield }
Indorsee of Jn[o] Hunton }
vs }
Edward Loyd Wailes }
Levin Wailes }

The Same Jury as in the above case.

We find for the plaintiff Two Hundred & thirteen dollars, Seventy one Cents.

Joshua Tyner, F. M.

Garland Wingfield }
Indorsee of Jn[o] Hunton }
vs } Debt
Edward Lloyd Wailes }

the Same Jury as above.

we find for the plaintiff the Sum of one hundred Twelve dollars, Sixty Seven and one half Cents, with Costs.

Joshua Tyner, F. M.

John Waller }
vs }
William Allen }
R. Middleton }
James Banks }

The Same Jury as in the Three last cases.

We the Jury find for the plaintiff Two Hundred & Seventy one dollars and Ninety Eight Cents, with Interest and Cost.

Joshua Tyner, F. M.

The Court then Adjourned Till Tomorrow Nine O'Clock.

Wednesday 11th [122]

The Court met pursuant to Adjournment.

Present as Yesterday.

John Heard }
vs } Case
Jarrard Walthall }

Jury Sworn, to wit.

1. Burket Green
2. Wm Carter
3. John Milligan
4. Wm Cross
5. Spencer Algood
6. Samuel Carr
7. Joshua Fields
8. Thomas Burges
9. John Smith
10. Eli Eavenson
11. John White
12. John McDonald

We the Jury find for the plaintiff the Sum of Sixty dollars, with Interest from the fifth day of May 1800.

Wm Carter, forn

John Crawford }
vs } Case
Richard Farr }

The Same Jury as in the above case.

We the Jury find for the plaintiff Eighty dollars, with Interest and Cost of Suit.

William Carter, F. M.

Forrester Upshaw }
vs } Debt
John Phain }
Charles Phair }

The Same Jury as in the above cases.

We the Jury find for the plaintiff Sixty Dollars, with Lawfull Interest & Cost.

Wm Carter, Foreman

Le Roy Pope }
vs } Case
Jno Cunningham }

I confess Judgt to Leroy Pope for one Hundred & Six dollars and Seventy eight cents, with Stay of Execution for Six Months.

John Cunningham

Joshua Tyner }
vs } Case
Jonathan Phair }

Refered and award returned as follows, to wit.

State of Georgia } We, the Arbitrators, chosen to Settle the dispute Between Jonathan Phair and
Elbert County } Joshua Tyner, have brought in our award, that the said Jonathan Phair ~~and~~ do pay the Said Joshua Tyner the Sum of fifty Six dollars, & he, the Said Phair, pay all costs that has accrued in all Said Suits that was between the Said Parties. Signed by us, the 21st day of October 1800.

L. McCurry, S. McAlpin
Wm Higginbotham, Wm Banks
M. Fleming, Jas Alexander

Patrick Peace }
vs }
Archibald Douglas }

Elbert Inferior Court

We agree to Leave all Matters in dispute in the above case to the final arbitrament & award of Richard Easter & Lewis Sales, with power of Empirage the award to

—

be returned to the Next Court. fourteenth October 1800. [123]

P. Peace, A. Douglas

Julius Howard }
vs }
Evan Ragland }

The Same Jury as in the Case Upshaw vs Jno & Ch^s^ Phair.

We the Juryers find for the plaintiff four hundred and Twenty eight dollars and fifty eight, with cost of Suit.

John Millican, Foreman

Woods & Lindsay }
vs } Judgment
Robert Kennedy }

Thomas Howell, the Bail below, Came into Court and Surrendered his Principal.

Nancy Hudson }
& N. Hudson }
vs } Debt
Robert Huddleston }
Joseph Huddleston }
Charles Goss }

I confess Judgment to the plaintiff for the Sum of Two Hundred & Thirty dollars, with Interest & Cost of Suit, with Stay of Execution till the first day of October next.

Robert Huddleston, Joseph Huddleston

John Andrew }
vs } Case
Jesse Tatum }

I confess Judgment to the plff for forty Nine dollars& forty nine & an half cents, with Stay of Execution till the first day of September Next.

Tait Plff

—

John Henderson }
vs } Case
Wm Carter }

The Same Jury as in the case Waller vs Allen.

We the Jury find for the plaintiff one Hundred and Twenty Nine Dollars and Ninety Cents, with Lawfull Interest & Cost.

Joshua Tyner, for^n

John Middleton }
vs } Case
William Martin }

The Same Jury as in the above case.

We find for the Plaintiff the Sum of one Hundred & Sixty dollars, with Interest from the 24th day February 1800, and Cost.

Joshua Tyner, fo^m

I acknowledge myself bound for the Stay of Execution according to Law.

James X Martin his mark

On the Petition of Randolph McDonald praying that his poll Tax be remitted.

Ordered, that the Same be Granted.

John Middleton }
vs } Cas
James Martin }

the Same Jury as in the case John Middleton vs William Martin.

We the Jury find for the Plaintiff the Sum of fifty dollars and Seven Cents, with Interest & Cost of Suit.

Joshua Tyner, Foreman

I acknowledge myself bound according to Law.

William X Martin his mark

Reason & Pope, assee }
vs }
James Kidd } [124]

The Jury as in case Waller vs Allen et al.

We find for the plaintiff Three Hundred and Ninety five Dollars and Ninety Six Cents, and Cost.

Joshua Tyner, foreman

John Allbritten, being brought in to Court for disorderly Behavior in the Court Yard, and he continuing refractory.

Ordered, that the Said John Allbritten be confined in the Stocks for the Space of Thirty Minutes.

Thomas Hudson }
vs }
Gabriel Higginbotham }

Jury Sworn, to wit.

1. Burket Green
2. Wm Carter
3. John Milligan
4. William Cross
5. Spencer Algood
6. Samuel Carr
7. Joshua fields
8. Thomas Burges
9. John Smith
10. Eli Eavenson
11. Luke White
12. Siah Cook

We the jury find for the Plaintiff Sixty Seven dollars, with Interest & cost of Suit.

John Millican, F. M.

Royal Norris }
vs }
A. Little }

Setled.

Woods & Lindsay }
vs }
W. Blankingship }

Jury Sworn, to wit.

1. J. Tyner
2. William Arnold
3. Henry White
4. A. McGuire
5. Henry Lawson
6. Jno Rowsey
7. John Murrah
8. A. Little
9. Toren Merrit
10. Ja^{s} Vineyard
11. John Nelms
12. Thomas Burton

We find plaintiff Two Hundred & eight dollars, Ninety Nine & three quarters, with Interest and cost.

Joshua Tyner, F. M.

Thomas Peter Carnes }
vs }
George Anderson }
& Peter Wyche }

Same Jury as above.

We find for the Defendant, Costs of Suit.

Joshua Tyner, F. M.

Memorable Walker }
vs }
Daniel Waller }

in this case, the Issue of Travers is with drawn by Plaintiff.

W^{ms} Newton }
vs }
Robert Martin, Senr }
Robert Martin }

In this case, Samuel N. Bayley comes into Court and acknowledged himself Special Bail for the defendants upon the usuel Terms.

Thomas B. Scott, William Allen, Wm Hightower came into Open Court & acknowledged them Selves Indebted to the Governor, for the time being, His Successors in office in the Sum of

five hundred Dollars, to be Void on Condition, that Robert Crump be & appear at the [125]
Next Superior Court to be held in & for this County & Not depart without Leave & in the mean time Keep the peace Towards all persons Whatsoever.

Thomas B. Scott, William Allen

Thursday 12th

The Court met pursuant to Adjournment.

Woods & Lindsay }
vs } Case
Charles Elles }

Jury Sworn, to wit.

1. John Smith
2. John Rowsey
3. Thomas Burges
4. Burket Green
5. Eli Eavenson
6. L. Smith
7. Wm Speers
8. Wm Carter
9. Benjamin Brown
10. Samuel Paxton
11. Charles Gordan
12. William Crittendon

We the Jury find for the plaintiff Thirty three dollars, Thirty one cents.

Saml Paxton

Woods & Lindsay }
vs }
James Flood }

The Same Jury as above.

We find for the plaintiff Thirty Seven dollars and Ninety Cents, with Interest & Cost.

Saml Paxton, Fom

Woods & Lindsay }
vs }
W. Blankingship }

I confess Judgment for forty two dollars, ninety three cents ¾ with Interest & cost.

Tait, Plff

Woods & Lindsay }
vs } Debt
William Guy }

The Same Jury as in the case Woods & Lindsay vs Charles Ellis.

We the Jury find the Plaintiff Sixty five dollars, Twenty Cents, with Interest.

Sam[l] Paxton

William Newton }
vs } Case
Robert Martin }

Same Jury as in the above case.

We the Jury find for The plaintiff fifty four dollars, Thirty five cents.

Samuel Paxton, F. M.

Ordered, That the following persons be appointed Constables (to wit)

Benjamin Allen, for Cap[t] W[m] Allen's District, John Royal, for Cap[t] Nath[l] Hudson's district, on their Complying with their Requests of the Law. Also, Hugh Means, for Cap[t] Martin's District.

Peter Johnson }
vs }
W[m] McGuire }
Thomas McGuire }

Setled, defendants cost.

On the Petition of Robert L. Tait and Thomas Oliver praying that they might Obtain Tavern Licence for the present year at their respective Dwelling houses.

Ordered, that the Same be Granted, on their complying with the law in Such cases made & provided.

Woods & Lindsay }
vs }
Gabriel Higginbotham } [126]

fi fa from the Inferior Court Levied upon real Estate, property claimed by Wm Crittenden, consented by council on both Sides to remove the Case to the Superior.

J. M. Dooley, Plff
C. Tait

Levillee & Brux }
vs } Case
Martin Dye }
Elisha Towns }

Setled.

Benjamin Porter }
vs }
Moses Mills }

Settled.

Reuben Lindsay }
vs }
Michael Coleman }

Settled.

Francis Gaddy }
vs }
William Reynold }

Settled.

John Andrew }
vs } Case
Joseph Pulliam }

Settled.

James Coleman }
vs }
Thomas H. Burton}

Settled, Defendants cost.

Jesse White }
vs } Case
Charles Goss }

Settled, Mutual cost.

Rountree & Taylor }
vs } Case
Martin Dye }

Settled.

Samuel Self }
vs }
Wm H. Davis }

Settled.

The Court proceeded to appoint Justices for the following Districts, to wit. Thomas Fortson & James Alston for Capt Alston District, Archalus Jarrett in Capt Jarrett District, Hugh McDonald in Capt Morrisons District, in lue of Elijah Oowens, Removed, Solomon McAlpin in Capt Montgomery District, in lue of Jonathan Phair, Removed.

Ordered, that James Huff be appointed Constable in Capt Jarratt Company, Samuel Paxton in Capt Alstons Company, William Post in Capt Blake Company, on their complying with the Law.

Wm Barnett, R. Hunt, R. Banks, S. Higginbotham

May 11th 1801 [127]

Preasant, Samuel Higginbotham, Esquire

Jurors Drawn to Serve at the next Term, to wit.

1. Wm Moon, Senr
2. Oliver Rock
3. John Wilson
4. Alex^r King
5. George Anderson
6. John Patterson
7. Lewis Gaar

27. James Brady
28. Samuel Nelson
29. Richd Sweezie
30. Benjamin Springer
31. Edmond Rowsey
32. John Cameron
33. John Craft

8. Thomas Briant
9. James Higginbotham
10. Wm Whaley
11. James Jarvis
12. Shelton White
13. John Shelton
14. Adley Alexander
15. Charles Fain
16. Wm Cunningham
17. James Manning
18. Robert McDole
19. Reuben Cook
20. Vollentine Smith
21. James Butler
22. Arthur Jones
23. James Kidd
24. Martin Sims
25. John Gober
26. Thomas Jones
34. Benjamin Goss
35. Benjamin Hearndon
36. Frances Powell
37. John Brewer
38. Wm Bradley
39. Robert Lowrymore
40. Nathan Jones
41. Andrew McEver
42. George Greenwood
43. Nathan Childs
44. David McCurdy
45. Robert Moseley
46. John Carson
47. John Cleveland
48. Wm Dudley
49. Daniel Parker
50. William Brown
51. Watson Dudley
52. Thomas Turman

At an Inferior Court held at Elbert Court House, the 13th day of July 1801.

Preasant, Wm Barnett, R. Hunt, R. Banks, S. Higginbotham, Esquires

David Witt }
vs } Case
Jno M. Whitney }

Dismised.

Archibald Clayton }
vs } Case
Elisha Brewer }

Jury Sworn, to wit. N° 1

1. William Moon
2. Robert McDowell
3. Reuben Cook
4. James Butler
5. Arthur Jones
6. Thomas Jones
7. John Carson
8. Frances Powell
9. Nathan Childs
10. John Craft
11. William Brown
12. Watson Dudley

We the Jury find for the defendant.

Wm Brown, F. M.

Gibson Sotherton }
vs }
George & E. Cook Admrs }

The defendants confesses Judgment to the plaintiff Ten Dollars, with Cost of Suit.

July 13, 1801 G. & E. Cook

On Motion of Charles Witt, praying that his poll Tax may be remited in Consequence of [128]
his Infirmity. Ordered, that the Same be Granted.

John Millican }
vs } Covt
William Bradley}

Jury No 1

We the Jury find for the plaintiff one Hundred & fifty Eight dollars & forty Cents.

Wm Brown, F. M.

Rountree & Taylor }
vs } Issue of Travisse
Leonard Turman }

Jury No 1

Discontinued.

John Hunton }
vs }
Edward Walthall }

Jury No 1

We find for the defendant.

Wm Brown

Appeal by Consent and the Cost to follow the event of Suit.

John Andrew }
vs } Att[t]
Jn[o] Wingfield }

Issue of Travisse

Jury Sworn, to wit. N[o] 2

1. W[m] Dudley	7. Amos Richardson
2. Edm[d] Rowsey	8. Silvanus Stokes
3. James Higginbotham	9. Rich[d] Bonds
4. Andrew McKever	10. John Lyon
5. John Smith	11. Henry White
6. John Boothe	12. James Sutton

We the Jury find for the Defendant.

W[m] Dudley

Woods & Lindsay }
vs }
John S. Head }

Thomas Head, the Bail below, Came into Court and Surrendered his principal.

When Silvanus Stokes Came into Court, with the defendant and acknowledged themselves bound to the plaintiff in Double the Sum mentioned in the Sheriffs Bail Bond, Conditioned, that if the defendant Should be Cast, that he, the Defendant, will pay the Condemnation Money, or Surrender himself as the Law directs, or I will do it for him.

John S. Head, S. C Stokes his mark

Woods & Lindsay } vs } Middleton Fanning }

Woods & Lindsay } vs } M. Fanning }

The Bail below Came into Court and Surrendered his principal, when John Craft, Came in and acknowledged themselves bound unto the plaintiff, in Double the Sum mentioned in the Sheriffs Bail bonds, Conditioned, that if the defendants Should be Cast, that he, the defendant, will pay the Condemnation Money, or Surrender himself as the Law directs, Or we will do it for him.

M. X Fanning his mark
John Craft

Le Roy Pope }
vs } Case
Frances Powell }

We Confess Judgment for Thirty four dollars, Twenty Two Cents, with Interest and Cost.

Francis Powell

Charles Parks } [129]
vs }
Jonathan Phair }

Jury N° 2

We the Jury find for the plaintiff Twenty one dollars fifty Cents.

Wm Dudley

Ordered, that the appointment of Inspectors at Olivers & Watkins Tobacco Inspections at Petersburg be Continued as made in July Term 1800.

The Court then adjourned untill nine O'Clock To morrow.

Tuesday 14th

The Court met pursuant to adjournment.

Present, as Yesterday.

Robert Martin }
vs }
Wm Newton }
Memo^ble^ Walker }

Jury Sworn, to wit. N° 1

1. James Butler
2. Nathan Childs
3. William Brown
4. John Lyon
7. James Sutton
8. Martin Turman
9. Robert Tait
10. George F. Gerrald

5. Andrew McEver
6. Robert McDowell
11. Reuben Cook
12. John Craft

We the Jury find for the ~~plaintiff~~ Defendant.

Wm Brown, Fore Man

George Cook }
vs } Case
Joseph Sale & }
Cornelius Sale }

The defendants Comes into Court, by A. Martin, their attorney, & confesses Judgment to the Plaintiff for the Sum of Two Hundred & Seventeen Dollars and fifty Cents, with Stay of Execution untill the fist day of January Next. 14th July 1801

A. Martin, Def^t Att^y

Wm Newton }
vs } Case
Robert Martin, Senr }
Robert Martin, Junr }

I Confess Judgment for the Sum of Eighty dollars, with Interest and Cost, Stay of untill the Second Monday in October Next.

J. Shackleford, Def^t Att^y

Dudley Jones }
vs } Case
John Hawthorn }

I Confess Judgment for Sixty dollars, with Interest & Cost of Suit.

Charles Tait, Def^t Att^y

John Hawthorn, Junr acknowledged himself Security, according to Law.

John Hawthorn, Jn^r

Woods & Lindsay }
vs } Case
Richard Farr }

Jury N° 1

We the Jury find for the plaintiff Sixty Six dollars, Ten Cents.

Wm Brown, for^n^

Samuel Watkins & C° }
vs } Case
William Smith } [130]

Jury N° 2

Sworn, to wit.

1. William Dudley
2. Watson Dudley
3. John Carson
4. Arthur Jones
5. James Hannah
6. Thomas Wooldridge
7. Littleton Johnson
8. William Robins
9. Henry Lyons
10. Wm Hatcher
11. James Higginbotham
12. Edmond Rowsey

We the Jury find for the Plaintiff fifty Six dollars & forty Cents.

Wm Hatcher

Wm Chisolm }
vs } Case
Syrus Jones & }
Siah Hendricks }

Jury N° 1

We the Jury find for the Plaintiff Eighty dollars, with Interest.

Wm Brown

Wm Falkner }
vs } Case
John Sweezie }
Henry Gatewood }

Jury N° 1

We the Jury find for the Plaintiff Seventy five dollars, with Interest.

Wm Brown

John Brawner Came into Court & acknowledge himself Security for Stay of levy according to Law.

John Brawner

Wm Hightower }
vs } Case
Geo. Greenwood }
B. Greenwood }

Jury No 2

We the Jury find for the plaintiff Eighty Six dollars and fifty Cents, with Interest.

Wm Hatcher, forn

Archibald Burden }
vs } Case
James Kidd }

I Confess Judgment in the above Case for Seventy Eight dollars forty Cents.

James Kidd

Thomas Akins }
vs } Case
Wommack Blankingship }
& Archibald Douglass }

The Defendants Comes into Court & Confesses Judgment for the Sum of fifty five dollars and Twenty five Cents, with a Stay untill the first day of December Next, with Cost of Suit. 14th July 1801

W. Blankingship, A. Douglas

Francis Carlisle }
execr of J. Ward, Decd }
vs } Case
Wm Goode }

I confess Judgment for the Sum of Two Hundred Dollars, with Interest ~~from~~ and Cost of Suit, with Stay of Execution till the Second Monday in February Next.

C. Tait, Deft Atty

Bridgar Haynie }
vs }
Maynward Colley }

Jury No 1

We the Jury find for the plaintiff Two Hundred Dollars, with Interest.

Wm Brown

John Watkins }
vs } Case
Charles Ellis }
John Ellis }

Jury No 2

We the Jury find for the plaintiff forty three dollars, thirty Seven Cents, with Interest.

Wm Hatcher

Wm Hightower } [131]
vs } Case
Reuben Easton }

Jury No 1

We the Jury find for the Plaintiff One Hundred & Twenty Six dollars, thirty Seven & a half Cents.

Wm Brown

John & Elisha Brewer }
vs }
Robert L. Tait }

Dismised.

James Sutton }
vs }
James H. Kidd & }
Robert Huddleston }

Jury N° 2

We the Jury find for the plaintiff the Sum of Two Hundred and Thirty one dollars, with Interest & Cost of Suit.

Wm Hatcher

Ordered, That the Inspections at Cold Water Tobacco Inspections be Continued, and at all other Inspections where the appoint is not particularly made at this Term to Continue as the year Last Past.

Index

www.ingramcontent.com/pod-product-compliance
Lightning Source LLC
Chambersburg PA
CBHW060452290526
45791CB00001B/79
* 9 7 8 0 8 0 6 3 5 7 8 3 6 *